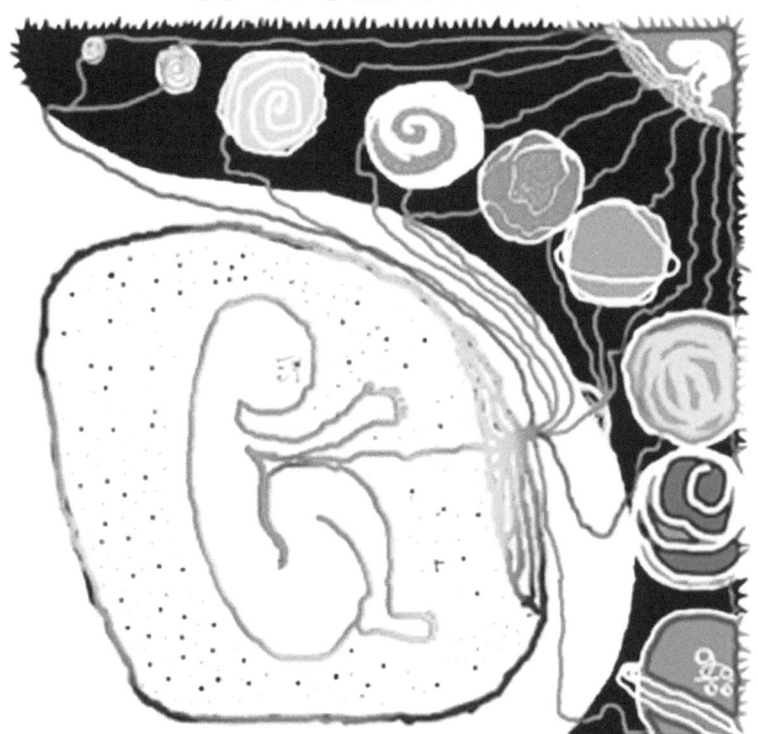

Published with *love* by Bënü Publishing™

an Entity of A Phoenix Rising Wellness Institute. (APRWI)

© 2007 Tisa Farrell Muhammad

No part of this book may be reproduced, stored in a retrieval system or transmitted by any means without the written permission of the author. All rights reserved.

9 stäges of WömbManHood: Poetic Anthologies of Shë

ISBN: 978-1-926436-04-3

ISBN EAN13: 1-926436-04-0

First Edition August 2014

For More Information:

www.benupublishing.com

For my mother, Joan Eliza Gabriel Farrell, my Aunts, My Daughters & the other significant women in my life who have taught me how to smile, pray & grow, this is dedicated to you.

If a caged bird isn't singing for love, it's singing in a rage.
　　　　　　　　　　　~Corsican proverb

IN ÄPPRËCIÄTION

For the Creator of the Wombniverse[1] who set me free,
for my Mother who birthed me and Father who protected me, and Sister Phipps who named me, and the women, my grandmothers, who taught me to love the herbs and make them into medicines,
and the men who were honorable enough to be my grandfathers,
who were warriors, in whose spirit I contend,
And the women who served as my spiritual mothers,
and the men who served as my spiritual fathers,
and the religion that taught me to love myself and be myself,
and the women who taught me how to be a sister,
through being my sisters,
and the three men who are my brothers and love me,
and those who are not but have acted as brothers, unconditionally,
and the man who I married and made me a mother,
and those that I love who made me a lover…
For the children I bore, for whom this was done for,
I thank you for doing what you have done,
Thus- I write these words in appreciation…
Love, Respect, Guidance, Forever Yours…

~Tifa

---

[1] *Wombniverse: a term i coined in 1999, denoting the Macrocosmic expression of femininity in the Uni-verse that imitates the triple-darkness of the Microcosmic womb found in all "WombMen".

Ä Message to All Wömbmen…

Ärise!
Bë Rënewed!
Frëë Yourself!
Bë Yourself!

FOREWORD

We Womb Workers exist in many clans, tribes and circles.

We are a United Nations of Women who live

a Healing Path.

We are women who mend the brokenhearted,

Women who mend the broken bodies,

Women who mend the broken spirits.

Our steady journey is to restore and rebirth ourselves

and others to Wellness.

We are grass roots and we are mainstream.

We are freedom fighters and Peace makers

and the liberators who will birth a Wholistic Humanity.

We are an Ocean of Women.

We are the Womb Workers.

~Queen Afua~

"Dr. Tisa Farrell-Muhammad is a Womb Worker and a Woman of Wisdom. Her book, 9 stages of WömbManHood: Poetic Anthologies of Shë, is a masterpiece of "Wombniverse Wisdom". By experiencing her poetry and art, one can join Tisa on the path of healing and wholeness. Give thanks to the Creator for Tisa and her work!"

Queen Afua[2]

July, 2008

---

[2] Queen Afua is an internationally renowned holistic specialist and author of the best-sellers: "Heal Thyself For Health and Longevity" and "Sacred Woman: A Guide to Healing the Feminine Body, Mind, and Spirit," "THE CITY OF WELLNESS: Restoring Your Health Through The Seven Kitchens Of Consciousness", "Circle of Wellness Journal", and her most recent release, "Overcoming an Angry Vagina: Journey to Womb Wellness". The Queen Afua Wellness Institute is evolving from her thirty-year-old business: Heal Thyself in Brooklyn, N.Y.

INTRÖDUCTION

In this millennium of "Sacred Women"- thanks to the inspired writings (and words) of such powerful women as *Mother Tynnetta Muhammad, Minister Ava Muhammad, Francis Cress Welsing, Queen Afua* and *Queen Mother Moore*- to name a few- we have no choice as sacred "wombmen", but to follow suit and rise beyond the confines of our own limitations.

These words are a true, yet incomplete compilation of my spirit during different stages of my personal evolutionary, revolutionary womb journey… I share my thoughts, some toxic, others healing, as a true balance and expression for and of myself. I pray that in it you may see yourself. Although many of these pieces no longer reflect my current thoughts, I still feel the importance of sharing them, knowing that my journey through life has had its difficulties, but through those trials I have found myself to be purified. The struggle continues, but in the meantime, continue to rise & grow. Never forgetting from whence you came, so that you will know where you are going. :)

9 stages of WömbManHood: Poetic Anthologies of Shë, is quite simply, my own tribute to the "Shë" in Më, You & Wë!~

I remain,
Your Sistar in the Cause of Freedom, Justice, Equality & Peace!

10/9/2007 @ 1:24:19 PM EST – 10/9/2014 @ 9:33AM EST

WŌRDS OF ENCŌURAGEMENT FRŌM MY MŌTHER

September 8th, 2014

The book of Proverbs stresses WISDOM. "Wisdom" is of God- Who is the Creator of ALL. 9 stages of WombManHood: Poetic Anthologies of She, encourages us to look more closely at the Creator from whom we were formed and fashioned to live for our short time here on Earth. As we reflect, it will do us well to begin our day meditating on at least one chapter of this book of Proverbs each day. At the end of a thirty-one day month, you and others would be blessed.

My five favorites are as follows:
1. Proverbs 14:27: "The fear of the Lord is the fountain of life…"
2. Proverbs 14:34: "Righteousness exalts a Nation, but sin is a reproach to any people"
3. Proverbs 14:1: "Every wise woman, buildeth her house, but the foolish plucks it down with her hands"
4. Proverbs 16:7: "When a man's ways pleaseth the Lord, he maketh even his enemies to be at peace with him"
5. Proverbs 16:3: "Commit thy works unto the Lord and thy thoughts shall be established"

The fifth is a prayer, which I wish for you, Tisa, as you launch the first of many more to come.

Love,

Mummy

LÕVE NÖTES.

It is such an honor to know a young woman like you. I see you as such an inspiration to woman of all ages. Your book is a must read. Your book is awesome, I feel you deeply. Being able to read about feelings you've felt before or words you wish you had said can be a release, a healing.   I see you as a wonderful inspiration to woman of all ages and stages of their journey. I am so honored to know you.

Love,

Mother Shirlée Bannarn

Table of Contents

IN APPRECIATION IV

FOREWORD VI

INTRODUCTION VIII

WORDS OF ENCOURAGEMENT FROM IX

MY MOTHER IX

LOVE NOTES X

WHAT REAL MEN SAY ABOUT HER XVIII

1ST TRY8MISTER 1

1ST STAGE PRE CONCEPTION SELF CULTIVATION IN TRIPLE DARKNESS — 2

The Rush 4

13 to Life 7

UNotreal 9

2ND STAGE CONCEPTION IN UNITY — 11

One Nite 13

Cool Lips on My Back 14

Water 16

Sunday Love 18

The Tree 20

3RD STAGE MEIOSIS DIVIDED & WE FALL   22

I've Fallen   I Can't Get up 24

A Wife   His Doorway to Heaven 27

Black, Pregnant   Hated 28

Phone Tag 30

cloak and dagger 32

Curious Miss Kate 34

Shameless 43

2ND TRY & MISTER 45

4TH STAGE WEEK 14 IN CREATING HER OWN BACKBONE   46

Doe a Deer 48

Chain of Fools 50

The Day that Never Was 57

Untitled 1 59

Untitled 2 61

Black Brotha B.S. 63

You let him pull you down 66

Keisha 67

Dear Sister words of love 69

5TH STAGE IMMUNOLOGY BRINGING JUSTICE TO HER R HART   71

Early in the Morning 73

Devoid of Love 75

Woe to the Low 77

Requiem to a Thief Rape 79

The Happy Housewife 81

Fly Girl 83

Impressions 85

N.I.G.G.E.R. 88

J.O.U. 89

21st Century Freak 91

Thong Songs 95

6TH STAGE SELF DISCOVERY SMELLIN' MYSELF   97

If I could fly 99

Changes 101
God, is this Really Me 103
Summer Breeze 105
Raw UnKind 106
Violent Flow 107
Betrothal Betrayal 109
Growin' Pains 112
Mirror 114
Old Stories 118
Phoënix 120
Wake Up 122
Be True 124

3RD TRY8MISTER 126

7TH STAGE PERFECTION GETTIN' TO LOVE ME — 127

Self Improvement 129
Requiem to My Womb 130
My Lover Superstar 132

sing song 134
A Day of Promise 137
UnEntitled 140
Pendant of Fools 143
Wronged 147
The Mask 150
Ain't that Something 153
Inner Peace 157
Free to be   the handmaiden's journey 159
The fungus among us 161
Revolution 163
The Heart of the Wombniverse 165

| 8TH STAGE 36 WEEKS EX X INTERNAL CHAOS & INTERNAL GROWTH | 168 |

Unity   a Narrative 170
Is it possible 175
La La Land Yankee 177
It's a Dirty Shame 179

Look who's laughing now 181
Islam stole her daughter 184
Know Thyself 186
I too, share your vision 189

9TH STAGE COMPLETION BIRTH OF A GODDESS — 191

So Grateful 193
Blessed 196
Can You Feel it 199
Sacred Womb 201
Sacred Warrior 203
It's Morning Wake Up 205
The Time 208
Eye Want to 209
Shë Journey unfinished story 211

10TH STAGE AFTERBIRTH LOVING MY SACRED TWIN — 212

"When you takin' she back" 214
One 221

Ebony 223
The healer 225
Mine. reclaimin' my own 226
And. Be. 227
Ashé 229
The God in We 231
It's All Good 233
One Their Story 237
WÖMB WISDÖM 247
WRITE YOUR WÖMB WISDÖM HERE... 252
ÄBOUT SHË 253

What Real Men say About Her

"No Nation can rise any higher than its women."
~ The Most Hon. Elijah Muhammad

"The disrespect of women is the reason that the earth and the world is in the condition that it is in. There cannot be a new world except that there is a new and better understanding of the female, which will give us (men) a clearer understanding of self and above all a clearer understanding of Allah (God)."
~ Hon. Minister Louis Farrakhan

9 stages of WombManHood I

2 Poetic Anthologies of She

What does Shë Cultiväte in the darkness of

her wömb?

"She waits, unaware she is waiting

She hopes, thinking all is hopeless

She is lonely, and yet, She is not alone…"

9 stages of WombManHood 3

The Rush

When I wake up my every thought is you.
You have become a god to me,
Because my every thought is thee
What am I to do?

To think of how I laid to rest
Each thought of GOD I possessed
To encompass my overwrought and doomed abyss
With countless thoughts of YOU!
What can I do?

The flowers & the leaves form thee
The petals~ nappy locks-~
Smell of beeswax & Egyptian Musk
The leaves of trees shape your limbs
'specially when its autumn part mimics your very skin-
Brown like honeycomb and
Sweet like brown sugar-
See? My mind's possessed I figure
What will I do?

My very shoes remind me of you-
When the right's gone
What will the left do?
I ask myself in wonderment of losing you…
Shall I go on?

Who walks the road long with one side of shoe?!?

I yell into the blue sky's eye
I hear your answer in its
echo…echo…echo…
You seem confused as I

There's a "coldness" in being alone
I pull my jacket tighter and feel
your embrace become warm~
I walk entranced
As we both dance
Through a bitter night
So drone & weary I feel
As I realize I've walked singly through this night…
I've lost my zeal…

Where will I go?
What will I do?
Who can I call when all thoughts are YOU!?

I pick up the phone
And hear your deep tone
Consistent…
Persistent…

I dial~
And each number throbs a song of sweet caress
I drop the receiver

9 stages of WombManHood

And picture the last button drop from my dress
I'm falling apart
Because you are my drug
I'm feignin'
As my fingernails search through the rug
For a piece of you
To inhale your mustiness is all I can do!
I'm cryin'
You wipe away my pain
As I yell your name
I'm goin' INSANE!
Who can I run to hide from your face?
Is there a crevice in my brain
Un-invaded with your space?
I'm running in circles
I'm bouncin' into you
You pull me over and strap me
Now I'm through…

I'm hugging you-
My hands can't move away
I'm shaking-
 As you shake me into reality…

You're gone…
I'm alone…
And I've got a white jacket on!
~11/24/96
*Dedicated to Russell, aka "The Rush".

13 to Life

A prisoner of destiny & fate
I've got to break these chains without debate
Poverty & unemployment got me tied
Got pregnant before marriage-
Sorry, I lied…

Blue~
No clouds in my sky
Heat from the sun
Pain from this guy
Baby's kickin' my gut out
No win,
But gotta try
Out of school
No fool,
It's cool
Just gotta graduate on time
Pressure's blowing my mind
Fear of the unknown
And I've grown
one year older
Regression's my holder
~In block letters~
I fight to progress
But recess is my time to play

9 stages of WombManHood

Mommy?
I love my job

Mommy…
I have a duty to produce a solution
For this problem of hate
Without debate
That's why I'm a prisoner
Of destiny & fate.
~ 9/3/97

UNotreal

These were all women like me
They had the style of Goddesses
The look of Queens and
The speech of Kings…

We discussed our fate or destiny
As if we were in a dream
Strong talkin'!
Not missing a thing
Yet, there was emptiness there…
We were not as "together" as we thought

We had fears.
We had insecurities.
We wondered~
Why?
When?
Where?
What & How?
People liked us
We spoke about our ugliness as beauty
And smiled
When we should have frowned
We were upside down!
We laughed in company
& cried

9 stages of WombManHood

When no one was around
Lest it got to town
That we were weak-
Not strong,
We weren't right-
But wrong,

Since we thought we knew
What
We Didn't.
~ 2/24/01 @ 6:42PM

9 stages of WombManHood

She feels the warmth of love comin' on...

"I did not know that you were there,

I was doin' it alone, all along.

Then, one day, out of the blue,

you showed your face & smiled...

I've been a fool for you since then...

Can you feel me?!~

12 *Poetic Anthologies of She*

One Nite

My face contorts
Then, relaxes
I shiver more from the heat of the moment,
Than from the cool night breeze
That floats freely through the open window…
Tears stream from my eyes, as my lips swell
I watch your silhouette conform
Into the abyss of sleep,
Then, I begin to massage your back,
Your neck-
So open and tender-
Seems my resting spot,
There I play
Stroking, coaxing, kissing
You awaken, as I nibble on your ear
Your phallus emerges, and, like Isis,
I search for the one part of you
That fulfills the depth of my pleasure…
Then again,
We fly.
~ 7/2/99 @ 1:05 PM

Cool Lips on My Back

Cool running water is the feel of your lips on my back.
The memory is old,
The desire, *new*
Reflecting on the moment I first laid my eyes on you,
Like the dew of a morning in an ancient past,
I can still taste your mouth,
Kiss your nose,
Caress your neck
With my own
Then wish that was all there was to our encounter.
But who can forget the pain of yelling your name when you went insane
That nite?
And others before as I walked through your door-
Later, than most.
Am I to forget?
Would you wish that fear you saw in my eyes
On your mother, daughter or son?
Could the coolness of your lips
Fade the scars of a bruise?
Or heal the scars of my mind?
Now that we're apart,
Do you remember
The good times or the bad?
The happy, or sad?

The true balance of your repentance to me

Comes from your memory,
And mine-
But do we have the time?

I'll always love you for the way you made me feel
As we made love,
Just as much as I'll hate you
For raping me of myself,
My innocence
My body
My mind…
But take comfort in this fact-
I'll never forget the moment I first laid eyes on you,
Or the coolness of your lips
On my back.
~ 5/3/99

Water

That hot summer day when you first saw me
I was a cool glass of Evian with a *Coca-Cola* bottle shape…
Water refreshes…

You took a sip of me,
I allowed you to take a long drink.
You undressed me many times
Imbibed my bath water
And cooled your tongue on my back

You wanted me to be sexy-
I became sexy…
Water becomes the glass.

The more you drank of me
The drier I became to you
I've heard many sips you've taken from other glasses that pass…
But still I sit here waitin'
Hopin'
Scopin' your eyes
Wishin' I saw my reflection-
In those muddy pools of lies!
You dipped…
You sipped…
You had your fun.
Now,

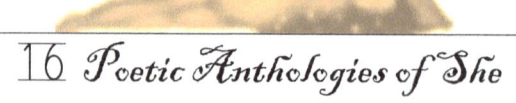

I'm carryin' your son
And you're callin' ME a HO?!?
I'm not your sip of tea no mo'?!?
I see…
I'm boiling.
You're…
Scalded.
~ 7/99

Sunday Love

They had that Sunday kind of love
The kind that we be dreamin' of
His kiss
To her, was as the delicate lips of a flower
The whiff of a rose after a sun shower-
He enjoyed her eyes
For in them lay no despise-
Nor lies-
As she had shared
Her sensitive thighs with him
And made him love.
He caressed her back with a loofah
And soaped all her troubles away
She washed his vulnerable feet
In baths of dead seas & brought them back to life-
She shed pounds of dried flesh off
Those heels & knees-
Vulnerabilities that he hid for years
After tears that flooded the fears of his denials
Yes, as the Blue Nile,
He cried her a river!
But the others-
We could not see
And let it be-
We had to meddle & pry in their "bizness"-
We had to tell funky lies

About what we thought we saw-
But didn't-
Until we caused their solidness to soften
Their stability to shake
Until in our faces they fell to pieces
We all shook our heads
As if it was a shame
But should have been ashamed
We stared at him & winked our eyes
Then glared at her & scowled our mouths
She went away one summer day
On a Sunday morning and never returned
He sat on his porch & watched her leave
Then drank a beer
Took a pistol
And flew away forever.
~ 6/20/01 @ 7:45PM C.S.T.

The Tree

We carved our initials in the tree
We said our love was meant to be
T + R = WE
And we are who we are…
We are love
Undying love
Pure love, Soft love
Love that has emotions
Love of untold notions
Love that has a heart
Love that is a start
Love that is a part
Of one love
Love, yes love
L-O-V-E ~spells "we"
We are if we be Ourselves
We are if we see Ourselves
We are if we grow against the flow
Against the know & *know*
That we are the purity
Found only in we
W-E-
Not he, she or it will not be
But you and me
That's the way to be successful
To do successful things

To fly on successful wings
And see success
Not the stress found in mess
That we can avoid.
We have children,
A girl & two boys
We are family
And like that tree
We will be *forever*
If we *never* forget
That you carved our initials
In that tree
T + R = We
And we *made love*
Because-
We *are love*.
~ 5/6/01 @ 8:15:11 PM to 8:31:13 PM

22 *Poetic Anthologies of She*

Who Am I?

"He called me into existence

They called me "Precious"

You called me "Beautiful"

While I called myself..."

9 stages of WombManHood

I've Fallen & I Can't Get up!

I would like to share a story with you
If we have time,
it might be two…
You seem surprised,
I've even seen you wipe your eyes…
In, shock?!?
How true…
As if you think me *dumb enough*
To have fallen in love with you!

You see,
You're used to communicating with fools,
Maybe not because you want to
But, nonetheless,
They're fools!
Especially if they fall for this here crap
You're sharing with me about
What you want
And what I may do for you…
Shoot! *You must think me dumb enough*
To fall in love with you!

What's that?
What did you say?
Is any of it true?
How quaint…

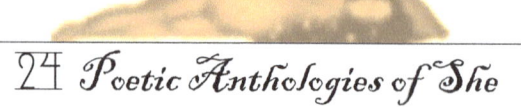

Of course, it's a lie,
'cuz I saw you wink your eye-
At your boys-
Yet,
I'm your "BOO,"
Damn!
You must think me dumb enough
To fall in love with you!

Why'd you take so long to come to the phone?!?
Who's over there with you?!?
Your MAMA?!?!?!
…thought you said she was dead!
Fi real?
You lied?
What's new?!
Boy! You need a slap upside your head-
Tryin' to drop a curse like that,
Sayin' your mama's dead…

So, *Can I meet her?*
No? Why not?
She's jealous of females dating her son?
I see~
I guess that includes me

Aiight bay-bee! Call me back, when she departs,
I can't wait to hear from you…
'Cuz now I've given you my heart,

I've forgotten *how dumb it was…*
To have fallen in love
With you.
~ 06/06/96

A Wife (His Doorway to Heaven)

A wife is not a girlfriend or a toy
A wife's your key to everlasting joy
Since she is the bearer of your seed
She has the honor of being the first to teach them to read

A wife, brotha!
Not a girlfriend or your toy
I'm Your Wife!

Only serious men need apply.
~ 12/5/98

Black, Pregnant & Hated[3]

No one likes a Black, pregnant woman!
They look at you like dirt
And treat you like *shit!*
There's no-"would you like a seat ma'am?"
Hell no!
It's "Stand you black ass up there bitch, and wait!
Aint nobody got you pregnant!"
'cuz no one likes a black, pregnant woman!

The worse for it are your own black "men,"
The selfish SOB's!
They won't offer you a hand-
As they push by you and try to get
On the other side of the store
The nigger could have used the next door!
But no one likes a black, pregnant woman…

You work hard for everybody!
Give a dime to anybody!
Offer tips to strangers…
But when you're pregnant-
You're dangerous!
Don't nobody wanna ass-ociate-
Affiliate

---

[3] This was written one day, on the bus home after having finally gotten a seat, while I was pregnant, Black & feeling sho' nuf hated. Some of us can relate…. :o)

Or be down
Hell they prefer to kick you around!
Since no one likes a black, pregnant woman!

But, I'll survive
I've made it this far through hell
Yet I'm still alive
I'll struggle up the steps
And still get ready fast!
I'll run you a marathon
On these two heavy legs
I'll cook my food
And rub my feet!
I'll even help you down the street
Since I'm a black, pregnant woman
And don't no-body like me!
~ 10/5/97

Phone Tag

The phone rang…
Ring…
Ring…
Ring…
Ding! It doesn't take a scientist to see
So why are you tryin' to fool me?
"Who was that guy?" I start to ask-
"Nonayabiznez!" you reply.
The words he used-
Loud flamin' air-
Could not be shielded by the phone
Pressed tightly to your ear
"Who's Sheila?"
I repeat to your reply
"Nobody"
She must be "somebody" to that guy (and to you, since you gotta lie!)
"I'll press redial, if you don't say!"
"I'll bust your lip! Now go away!"
"I pay that bill!"
"Who gives a damn? You'd pay more if I weren't your man!"
Pause…
The phone rings…
Ring…
Ring…
Ring…
Ring…

Poetic Anthologies of She

At it we stare,
Afraid to answer,
Yet, wondering who's there?
The answering machine picks up…
Inhale…
"Hey baby, its mama! Just calling to check up on ya'll…
Hate I missed you… I'll call later…"
Click.
Exhale…
Oh, such foolish games we play…
I press redial as you walk away.
~ *"Drama" coming to a Theatre near you.*
…To be Continued…
~ 7/2/99 @ 2:45pm

cloak-and-dagger

Your hold was so cold
Was that a hug?
Because I felt a painful tug
Of electricity shoot through my heart.
Your motions are, *loving*
But your *e*-motions-
Deeper streams of ice-
Cause me to shiver from this hatred I feel…
You are studying me
And my every move, as if, with *love*
But your eyes~ burning coals of fire on my skin~
Cause my flesh to *bubble & singe*
You lay next to me as an enemy
You laugh & mock my words-
Although sincere-
To you
They're foolish ramblings of fear…
You move to strike as a snake in tall grass
Your arms coil around me
Constricting my breath
"I-CAN'T-BREATH!,"
I scream in pain
You flick your tongue into my ear
Then slowly *hisssss* my name
You lunge a kiss at my cheek
As venomous as your bite

Then, thirsty, suck on my neck …
I stare into burnt eyes of hell
Then realize
That you don't know-
That I know-
That you
Don't love me.
~ 10/3/00

Curious Miss Kate [4]

Curiosity bent Miss Kate
But satisfaction made her straight.
Yes sir! Miss Kate was an *enquiring* mind
She wanted to know-
And she *sho' nuf* found out!
There was no question she was not going to ask
There was no mountain
She was not going to climb
No rock she would not turn
Just to answer the questions
In her dilapidated mind!
She lay in bed-
At night-
Obsessed with anger at the moon
That shone so delicately in her room
For that was the only thing that stopped her
From calling whomever
She wanted to harass with her last enquiry…
When the sun arose
And the time was kosher
She would be out that door
And standing on some floor

---

[4] My beloved brother Toussaint read this piece and commented that it could very well be an attack on the *Paparazzi*, since it was written during a time of severe criticism of them and their alleged involvement with the death of Princess Diana, etc. To me, it is my own expressed opinion of people who seem to always want to *know about everybody else's business*, but their own. What do you think?

In an unknown location
To ask
And ask
And ask!…
To no avail
Would they tell
But yet, she would use
Their tale as her personal sell
Endless stories were written
About fibs & lies
And yet these satisfied Miss Kate
For she was an enquiring mind
And she had to know!
To any lengths would she go-
To find who was in the know-
Whether or not they knew any thing at all!
She sat up late pounding
On any keyboard
That was not worn
Or torn
By her possessive,
Obsessive, mind
Searching through
Innumerable Articles to find-
The "TRUTH"!
She traveled on highways
And byways
And freeways
Past seaways

To see ways
And find ways
To pick some one's mouth
To stick some one out
To prick some one's mind
And possibly find
What they would share
In kindness with her…
But they all seemed to miss her
Or Miss Kate them
For in this business-
Of other people's business-
You had no friend
And that was to be
To her own
Detrimental end
For on one of her tangential
Quests for fame
She asked for a name
That belonged to the same
Person she had hounded
For years
And with tears
And new fears
Although they spared
Her the horror-
Of a beat down-
They told her
To settle down

As they brought her
A gown
Stained with blood
Stained with mud
Stained with crud
Oooo Stinky
Was all she could think
As her excited pinky
Bobbed up and down
Filling her pad
With details
Of what she thought she saw…
Until they rested
The gown on the floor
At her feet.
All neat.
And sweet.
They curled that gown
That blood stained
Mud stained
Crud stained
Stinky gown
Causing Miss Kate
To frown
The old lady who
Was kind enough to invite her in
To fulfill her curious enquiry
Was the same
To label her with the sin

Of being the cause-
Of that gown's effect-
For it was her mouth
That stained
The name
Of the woman of fame
Who once wore that gown
Around
Her home
On quiet evenings
In the morning
Sitting on the porch
At sunrise
And at sunsets
At times when-
She welcomed the moonlight-
For it was the only light
That shielded her
From the *enquiring minds*
Of millions
Who knew about
Her personal affairs-
Be they real or imagined-
They were Miss Kate's own words.
That gown witnessed
The night of the intrusion
The night of the illusion
The night of confusion
That could be heard-

For miles-
Around that town
As the woman of fame
With the slandered name
Ran for her life!
Out of her moonlit room
Into her garden of tended flowers
And mended bowers
And offended neighbors
Who watched her-
And helped to feed-
The stories to Miss Kate
Who had the *enquiring mind*
And *had to know…*
She crawled for her life
Among those flowers
And that fresh manure
That she delighted in pouring
Sparingly in each row
As much as Miss Kate
Delighted in smearing
Her manure across the faces
And pages-
Of millions-
Who read her Bullshit!
For in her knowing
She knew nothing!
The intruder recounted
To the lady with the bloodstained gown

A story about
Something he read
That said
She liked to be fed
By different men
At the same time
For she was the "Queen of Slime"
And he found it hard to find
That she was refusing
To let him feed her-
His gun-
Until he angrily
Realized
That Miss Kate
Was full of lies
And through his hate-
And her ill fate-
He had already shot her
But, it was too damn late
Before he came to that realization
For, by then, she was dead
But the words
That he had read
Were the words that Miss Kate said-
And there was no taking them back-
Nor bringing back the lady of fame
With the bloodstained gown
Who was innocently gunned down
Because Miss Kate had been around town,

Enquiring,
And wanting to know
What she knew not…
But now this home
Of the nice old lady
Became a furnace of fire
And guilt,
And, the sofa that served
To comfort her
Was a cushion of pins
Razor sharp & Venomous
On her buttocks
She couldn't get
Out of there fast enough!
Miss Kate ran with her life
Like the woman with the gown had run
Then,
She fell among weeds
And *dog shit*
Because of her own *bullshit*-
Smeared across the minds
Of millions
Who read her stories
Thinking she knew,
What she knew not
She got what she deserved-
For when the story of how
Miss Kate lay,
Moaning,

9 stages of WombManHood

In the grass that day-
Hit the press-
Her next article, was her last
For on that day
And for weeks to come
No one read her stories
They were too busy
Reading the stories
Written about her
From the people she hounded,
Searching to fulfill her desires for fame
By smearing others names
Yes sir!
Miss Kate was an *enquiring mind-*
She had to know-
Ah, yes~!
Curiosity bent her out of shape
But satisfaction got her straight!
~ 12/31/00 @ 8:53:59 AM to 9:53:19 AM

Shameless

She watches
She secretly watches
And waits
She sees
She knows
And she fears
For what she knows
Is not to be honored
It is quietly
Hidden
Secretly forbidden
Yet unspoken
For
If she is to say
Then it will be worse
Anyway
It will be harder
To be incognito
For they all will now know
That she is to be shunned
And hated
For what they have wanted
And waited for
She has received
Without even wanting it
Without asking for it

And for it
She is ashamed
For she is but a child
She is not a woman
She has a womb
But it is not sacred
It is to be spooned
And shared
And spared
Forgiveness
For
Although she is only a child
That's not enough
For her to not
Be molested.
~ 12/30/00 5:34:25 PM to 5:41:26 PM

Poetic Anthologies of She

9 stages of WombManHood 45

"You need to get more backbone" they said,
She couldn't see it, so, she couldn't believe it...

"I'm carryin' the weight of the ancestors on my shoulders"
Shë thinks, so now, she believes...

Doe a Deer

When a woman sees herself
She may one day see that locked within her chest
She bears the wounds *of others*…
At times she may fail to realize that she is the carrier
Of guilt imposed on her *by others*
She goes forward in life
Analyzing how she will be perceived
By *others*…
Occupying her mind
Lost in the expectation of *others*…
She does not have a goal
Others do…
She does not have a life~
It belongs to *others*…
She does not belong to herself-
She is the property of *others-*
Like that man that she passes in the street
Who feels like *she is teasing him* with her short skirt on
Or them *tight-ass* (shut yo mouth!) apple bottom jeans that she got from her Mama
Forcing him to have to grapple or rape her
Or, forcing herself to be raped (?) (Something *others* say at times like these…)
Or
The man or husband in her bed that rolls over at night
And expects her to fulfill his desires & needs
Irregardless if she is ready or even awake to oblige him or not
For she is his woman and *that is what a real woman would do…?*

So, on that note,
Others may insist that the buck stops there
But, I dare ask, Where does the buck *really stop?*
Certainly not at the pleas of the doe
For after all~
A doe is dumb.
~ 5/23/01 @ 3:50PM

Chain of Fools

She was a link
In his chain of fools
She devoted herself to him
Made him feel like a king
While she played
Court jester- then
Made everyone watching
Laugh-
As they knew she was nothing
To him but another toy…
She *sang* him songs
To help him sleep
Washed his back
And rubbed his feet
Paid all his bills~
"Outstanding"
And "Long Overdue"~
As if she were the wife
That he never knew
Remaining a link
In his chain
Of fools…
She stayed up
Long nights
Rethinking how to make him see

50 *Poetic Anthologies of She*

That-
She was still
His fantasy-
Island, where he could
Swim,
Find solace,
Play games,
And rest
A long sleep
Betwixt her breasts
But, somehow
Her plan failed to work
For, he would yawn
Then ask her to
"Please. Call back at dawn…"
She took that as a cue-
One day-
To cook him a meal
Of shrimp scampi
Cheese rolls,
Green beans,
And a bottle of 1947 *blah, blah, blah* Chardonnay
Then wrapped them
Delightfully
With silverware
She bought for whom
From *God knows where*
Then, drove it slowly
On her brakes-

So that her king
Might enjoy
And then partake-
Of her proposal
To be his wife
For better…
For worse…
For life…
She smiled, *then frowned* as she spotted
An unknown car
Parked in the driveway
New-
Without a scar-
A car that looked
Red
And pink
As a virgin's bed
Soft and curvy
As a woman's leg
A car that only a woman
Would own
With the license plate-
"CANDY"-
Nailed to its throne
She turned off her lights
To hide in the dark
So that she might watch
And see~
Who was parked?

Hours passed
The sun-
Arose-
While she waited
And watched
Without blinking
While thinking
And smelling
Her food
Stinking
Up her car
She chewed on a roll
Then feigned another
Until the whole Meal -
Was picked over-
As she watched
Her lovers' Lover,
Leave his home
Then, drive off
In the red
And pink car
With "CANDY"
Nailed to its throne.
Then,
She picked up
Her cell phone
And called…
"Hello?"
Said the voice, tired & strained,

"Hello." she replied
Her love feeling maimed
And destroyed
As he toyed with her
And told her a lie
Of how he stayed up late
With some guy
"Playing games
Watching movies
T'was groovy
While "sippin' on smoo-vies"
How he was tired
Dead, tired…
"Call me back, Baby…"
He said
"I wish I could talk, but *I'm still feelin' red…*"
He paused.
She waited for him to finish
So that she might think of how to say
That she had his meal made
 With a bottle of 1947 *blah, blah, blah* Chardonnay
Sitting with her
Here, in her car
Ragged,
Beat up,
Scarred…
Her car-
That needed a paint job-
Long, *long ago*

While she paid all his bills
Long over due
Her car-
That needed an oil change
New brakes & new tires-
And a personal plate
That said:
"FOOL"
But, it was too late…
He… hung… up…
She sat there
Long enough to accept
That *he was her man*
And *he was a man-*
And *men needed things…*
She sat there long enough-
To accept
That *he was her man*
And- she- loved- him
For better…
For worse…
For life…
As any wife-
Who was married to a
Wifeless man
She sat there, long enough to accept-
That he was her man
And since she *needed a man*
She was willing to stand

And be counted
As a link-
In his chain…
Of fools.

~ 1/9/01 8:00:41 AM to 8:52:50 AM

The Day that Never Was

I crave that touch-
Though sharpened tough
At night, I lay awake & yearn embrace,
'til you push me between the sheets
& tell me "MOVE!," you need your "space,"
So selfish you are,
Such roughened lace...
You smiled,
& yet a grimace I see,
As you asked,
"Will you marry me?"
If I knew then, what I know now,
I would have saved you that last bow,
Since your back hasn't broke since then,
Yet, on mine, your hands broke the skin.
I gaze off in these nights & see,
The cheer we shared, when I was free,
& now I walk-
A limp in part,
Wanting to fly-
a brand new start,
Alas, my gaze has dimmed since then-
The night we became more than friends...
And, if the hands of time could turn,
I'd back them up-
Past what I yearned,

Then, on that day of history's making-
The day we smiled & our eyes met-
Would never be,
For I'd have taken,
The long way home
& smiled alone,
'til now,
For, I'd be free.
~circa 1999

Untitled 1

Our separation pains me.
Our union hurt me even more.
I devoted myself wholly to you,
Solely to you,

Your mind stayed in gutters and behind *thong songs*
Watching Olympic beauties
Studying their frame with your game
In *innocent's* name-

I ask- What in the hell did you want me for?
I'm fairly- barely there
(you said it didn't matter where)
But you had to have your way----
And you did for a while.
You were the head of the house
Ahead of me in power,
When you told me to "Shut up!"
I shut up my grief behind pretentious smiles
And "yes sirs…"

The hoopla couldn't last long
For I had to be real…
But I guess you didn't feel
That one day I'd leave you-
Stranded & alone in our new home

So,
now you're free
To be who you wanna be-
A bachelor with a crib
A ride
Some green
& no damn sense!!
~ 10/1/00

Untitled 2

We are separate
because we could not start as a part of *The One*.
I left you because I don't deserve you,
Nor you me,
You see,
In our unit- there was no unity.

You didn't beat me.
I beat myself up with hatred
& low desires
& no esteem.
You didn't hurt me.
I hurt myself-
Alone on my throne of selfishness
Your selflessness could not survive
As my anger would thrive in the midst of my smiles
The miles we traveled could not erase
The base thoughts shone from beneath my face
& linked to my heart

We had to part,
for in your love I could not see-- me
Nor be free
Because I was
And will always be
My own enemy

Since I failed to realize that the key to loving you
Was by first
 Loving me.
~ 10/20/00

Black Brotha B.S.

Why did you end our conversation when we entered the bus?
We were having a good time discussing the plight of our people
How I could do something
And you could do something…
We were ready to start a revolution!
But you stopped talking when the bus came.

You quoted Farrakhan, Malcolm-*the* X and Assata Shakur
And how *we needed to become more like them…*
You had us ready to throw down our bottles & pick up our guns!
So why did it end when we got on the bus?

"Be Strong Sista!" you said,
"Fight Brotha!" I said back,
You smiled.
I smiled.
And Then…
The bus came.

You called me "baby"
And "sugar"
And said I looked "real good"
Then you invited me to sit my "brown sugar thighs" down
And tell you all about myself
And what "we could do 'lata'…"
I ignored you and sat up front.

9 stages of WombManHood

How you changed when we got on the bus...
Brotha?
What you are suffering from is known as "Black Brotha Buck" Syndrome
It's the type of dis-ease that strikes you when you least expect it
Clouds up the intellectual
And excites the sexual
Black Brotha "BS" is an infection that affects the brotha that's a soldier
As well as the bourgeoisie
It started in the sixties
When we integrated
And lost our focus watching "Super Fly"
And other *blaxploitation* flicks
Inspiring us to orgies and crude sexual acts
Yes, Cleopatra Jones- *you had something to do with it too!*
It had something to do with the dirty white hippies
Who chanted "Make love, Not War!"
As we chanted "Black Power!"
~*We mixed their agenda with ours*~
So here we sit on a bus
Me- Wondering why you'd humiliate me
And change our conversation-
It was so good-
Into this off beat mating dance
As if my intellect makes me a better lover
than some dumb, pointless sister in designer clothing...?

Then, it dawned on me.
You really don't mean any harm.
You just don't see any thing wrong with it.

In fact,
You would probably be more comfortable
Waking up next to me and pumping "Ice Cube"
Than you would next to some other sister.
On second thought~
I'm sure anyone could relate
To "Ice Cube" after a night of passion
With a brotha like you,
but, would any woman would do?
Why waste your body
And risk losing your mind?
Am I really that "good to go"?
Or are you just "hard up to find"?
Think about it next time I'm talkin' politics
And you're talkin' sex & tricks
Our Mission & Your Passion don't mix.
~6/14/96 @ 5PM

9 stages of WombManHood

You let him pull you down

You let him pull you down.
You should have stopped him from the gitgo
But you really didn't seem to know
That he would treat you like a "HO"
And call you *stupid*.

But that's just the beginning of the end
'Cuz when they dis' you
Then that's the same boyfriend that will beat you
Since you let him pull you down.

Now it's okay for him to treat you like trash
'Cuz you threw yourself out the door at him
Sold yourself to conquer sin
gave up your God
For nothing but hell
And now you know its' lost...
The respect is gone
Now he calls himself "BOSS"
Since you let him treat you like trash.

Love. It's not worth his dissin' you
Hate. It's what you feel for him.
Anger. At yourself for falling in love & losing your God.
You lost your God
To let him pull you down.
~ 8/28/96

Keisha [5]

Sis, what about this life had you feeling like you did?
What pain in this world made you take it all away?
I just heard about you
And the fact that you were loved
Was that not enough?
Your black skin should have been
Enough to soothe you
Your coal lips should have edged away
Ebbed away your hatred of self
Life
Your existence…
Keisha,
I knew you not
But sister,
I pain for you
I had not the opportunity to see
What you saw
But I know that nothing
In this world
Can justify
What you did to yourself
Your mother & yours…

---

[5] "Keisha" became a part of my life the morning that my father received a call from Sherona Hall (ancestor), telling him that her body was found hanging by her mother and sister in her home. She left a note blaming her mother for her demise & her decision to die in such a violent manner. She was still in her twenties…

You lie
Frozen
This morning
But in their hearts
There will always lie
The heat of haunting
Wondering
How they could have
Should have
Stopped you
Before it was too late…

Your mama's wishing
That she spent the nite next to you
So that she could have called for help
Found someone to help you
Loved you enough
More than she had ever done
To soothe you
And save you
So that today
The worst day of her life
Would be the best
For afterall,
You would still be here
Sis, what about this life,
Had you feelin' like you did?
~ 7/11/2001 @ 10:47 AM- 10:53 AM

Dear Sister (words of love)

Please be aware
& *beware* of all imposters
Please try to avoid
The void left by false love
Don't be bought or sold on the idea of care
Don't sell yourself cheap on one nite of passion in the back seat
You'll feel defeat
Lose much sleep
You may lose sight of sanity's light
If you don't fight the hurt or pain
Brought by the mention of his name
Keep up your head if you have fallen-
In & out of love in an instant
Walk upright with pride for
You are an *invincible woman*
You are God's gift to life
Despite the feelings of much strife
In your heart
Please don't start to be depressed
Or feel repressed…
Oppressed
Or messed on by his snickers of fun
Walk strong although alone
And *love* your son
You are the One
Who can end the cycle of madness

9 stages of WombManHood 69

His badness *was gladness*
Until he too got hurt
And abandoned by the one he loved
You are above that
In fact-
That child you call your son
Is watching you to see
If you too will leave
So cleave hard to each other
& Be a good mother
Don't try to smother
Him with the hate of ill fate
Just grow & create
With love & Love
Above all else
With love…
Dear sister.
~ 10/21/00

5th Stage
Immunology: Bringing Justice to He(r)Art

She prays, hoping He hears...

She waits, confident he'll appear...

"I didn't know I had one,

Until, you broke it."

72 Poetic Anthologies of She

Early in the Morning

It was so early in the morning
When you showed up here wanting to talk
The cock crowed twice
Before you suggested taking a walk…

The eggs were made
Before you fell out & lay in my bed
The toast was burned
Before you made me a sandwich instead

It was so early in the morning
When you showed up here wanting to talk
The cock crowed twice
Before you suggested taking a walk…
The juice was poured & drank through
Before you'd even say, *"Thank You"*
The oatmeal was soft & lazy
Before you even said, *"Baby"*

It was so early in the morning
When you showed up here wanting to talk
The cock crowed twice
Before you suggested taking a walk…

The shirts were pressed
Before you professed how much you were blessed

9 stages of WombManHood

The drapes were drawn
Before you were begging to stay here much longer

It was so early in the morning
When you showed up here wanting to talk
The cock crowed twice
Before you suggested taking a walk…

I was so weary by the time
You asked me to marry you…

I was too stressed by the time
You confessed you'd bought me that dress…

It was so early in the morning…
~ 4/23/01 7:00 AM to 7:23 AM

Devoid of Love

It's hard to give away love that you don't have.
I let you manipulate my body,
My mind
My time
Here I sit
Nameless
Graceless
Formless…
A mess of unloved flesh
Raped of its entirety.

It's hard to give away love that you don't have.
Why am I to judge who you are
By what you say?
I've judged wrong every time
As some sit & pine
Over my stupidity

It's hard to give away love that you don't have.
You held me
And claimed you loved me
I submitted to you
And unlocked my passion
Devotions of untold notions
Is what I've given…
To you…

It's hard to give away love that you don't have.
Insensitive piece of flesh you are
How many more before you were the same?
My game was always the same…
I searched for love.

It's hard to give away love that you don't have.
I prayed for peace~
Exposing myself to war~
Upheld divine principles
Hiding in *Shaitan's* door
Repent- I will
Before pushed through destruction's core
Now I sit
Crying
Mourning
In loss of love
Love I don't have…
In my pain
I realize that I must now *finally wait* on Allah.
 ~ 8/18/96

Woe to the Low

Woe to you woman of the darkness!
Woe to your sons,
Daughters,
Mothers,
Your fathers,
Woe to the way that you think
Because of your thoughts- we stink!

Woe to your friends-
Woman of low morals-
Because of your songs
We wail our laurels…

Woe to the men you marry!
For it is through their seed
And yours-
The earth is weary…

Woe to you night stalkers!
And pool hawkers
Who sit in wait victimizing our sons
And daughters
Spreading your legs apart to share your fruits
Hoping to arouse curiosity
With mere debauchery & filth
That you show

Yet to you…
If you but only knew
The damage you cause
You'd hide your head in shame
And cease the applause…

Woe to you woman of darkness!
It is by your act that we are raped
It is by your words that we are shaped
It is by your smile that we must frown
For it was you who pulled us down
You were to blame for destroying our name
Woe to you!
And to yours~
The same!
~ 11/23/00 @ 12:29:02 PM

Requiem to a Thief (Rape!)

How did you expect me to respond?
You took what did not belong to you-
That was mine.
I cherished it.
I marveled at it & how blessed I was to have it.
I planned on sharing it with someone dear to me,
Near to me…
Precious to me
You were none,
No, *not even one* of those people…
But you took it anyway!
You took what did not belong to you!
You thief!
Smilin' at me as if you know the value of what you possess!
A connoisseur of fine perfume couldn't even ascertain
The depth of the purity found in the flower-
My lotus of sacred love,
He would have handled it with such care-
You *ripped it apart-*
Stopped one step short of tearing the petals off!
With such gluttony you devoured what did not belong to you!
Just because I said "I do"
Should not have given you the right to do,
What you did…
I might carry your name but I cannot see
How I became *your property-*

And even if I was
How come you treat your ride with such pride,
Then kick me to the curb each time I'm near
Like a stray dog!?!
Why do you use me as an instrument of pleasure,
And fail to pay the measure of your share in child support?
You stole the most precious thing that I had...
You spread dis-ease to my womb
You contaminated my temple with false gods
You tore down the loom of my cocoon,
And have the nerve to sit here on this phone
& ask me to come home
so we can make LOVE!!!?!?!?!
Read my lips---
H-E-L-L NO!!!
~ 10/2/00

The Happy Housewife

She's the *happy* housewife.
By all observations her happiness is real.
She's the *happy* housewife,
But is this *sadness* that she feels?
How can it be that she has tears?
Stability has quenched her fears
And she's been married all these years-
So she must be the *happy* housewife.

How dare she speak about her problems?
Her friends have more than she!
She has a roof over her head…
So *happy* she must be!
But who can question what her mission is to be a *wife*?
It's what so many young girls strive for-
It's the "hook-up" for life!

"It's like the movies," they say,
she laughs at the thought,
For she's had drama *all these years-*
The romance was minimum to not-
"Three thumbs down, and a one flag salute!"
Has been her storyline,
But she's the *happy* housewife,
So who says that she minds?

9 stages of WombManHood

She's had these babies for her man
But that still is not enough to stand
Since no one's given her a hand
In doing her housework-
Since to her family she's *"Ms. Butterfly McQueen"*
A *"gotdamned mammy"* is what they mean-
Since she's the *happy* housewife,
And *"happy housewives"*
Aren't Black.
~ 7/5/00

Fly Girl

I've got to straighten this nappy head of mine
'cuz the kinks are just too much
And it's taking too much time…
'sides, I wanna get me a brotha
Who's too fine
Too fine
And these brothas
Got no time
For a *nigga-nappy* sister
With a kinky head like mine.
It's like if my butt ain't big enough
And my lips-
Too flat & wide
I've already got to wear blue contacts
To hide the brown inside
My skin's on the brink of black
And that's *too borderline*
And if it weren't for my *Hispanic side*
I wouldn't look this fine…
As for my legs-
Hate 'em! The muscles just too thick!
Old country livin' got me givin' hell
With my tight jeans,
Fittin' nice & slick
As for my head
It's just too much

9 stages of WombManHood

The kinks too tight- *no curl!*
They hold me back from looking
Out for a brotha to rock my world
I dyed it blond the edges white
So it'll look just so right
My weave blends in like it's a sin
Sewed in so tight-
Scalp would come out in a fight!
Ha ha ha!
Just laugh, I do!
'cuz you wish I was you, *envious of me you be!*
'cuz after I perm this nappy head of mine
That fine brotha you got on your arm,
Will be cooing
And staring
At me!
~ 7/18/1996 @ 10:15-10:35AM

Impressions

When I stopped impressing you
I became depressed.
There were no more *"good job's"* or *"magnificent's"*
Leaving those gorgeous lips…
You called me once in a *very blue moon*,
Just to make me feel that you still liked me
Or maybe not,
Who was to say
It didn't matter anyway…

So I got depressed.
Stopped washing myself as often as before-
Preferring instead to lie around-
Stare at the floor
Or simply open the door and peer out
Looking out thinking you would "drop by"
Or drop a line to tell me "hi"

Then time went by…
And by
And by,
And I,
Was still depressed
Unsure of how I could impress
My friends
And family

That looked down upon me
In shame
Or judged me
Or kept speakin' my name
On the phone
Or at family gatherings
That I refused to attend
Since I was unwilling to amend
Myself
And stop being depressed

The seasons changed from gold to cold
And still I lay around for untold
Months
Waiting to see if you would come-
You didn't.
Then,
I forgot why I became depressed
In the first place
Since so much time had passed
And my circumstances began to change
And the seasons changed from lean to green
And I began to see myself
Lying in a funk
Fi real
Since I hadn't taken a bath
in what seemed like years
And my cheeks had dried up all my tears
And my eyes had faded all my fears

And my thoughts began to grow
And flow into new rivers
Of promise
New horizons of new suns
With golden rays
Comforting me
Encouraging me
To be myself
And stop impressing
Others
And live.
And So,
I did.
~ 4/6/2006 9:09:47 AM

N.I.G.G.E.R.

N-I-G-G-E-R…
Etched deeply into an old hardwood desk.
NI-GA-GA-GERRRRR…
NIG-GERRRR…
The sound was old, but the lips were new,
The expression left no impression on the mind,
As it was just letters on the tongue,
One word like all, but all unlike the one…

NIG-GER!

I'm a nig-ger
You're a nig-ger
He's a nig-ger
She's a nig-ger
We are nig-gers
They are nig-gers

NIGG-ER… NIGG-ER…NIGGER!
HMMMM…
'SCUSE ME!
'SCUSE ME MISS?!
UHMN…
WHAT DOES THIS WORD MEAN?
~ 9/30/88 (a piece from back in the day…)

88 Poetic Anthologies of She

I.O.U.

Still waters run deep, deep, deep…
Shut eyes mimic sleep, sleep, sleep…
Pursed lips hide pain, pain, pain…
Flowing tears show shame, shame, shame…

Ay E, Ay E I O U,
And I don't know why?
Is it because you saw me with that guy?
Your jealousy is killing my love for you
I can't do a thing that you want me to
So why do you stay?
Is it because we committed to this day?
Then let's move on-
I can't stand singing this same song-
My feet are hurting me
And I can't stand long
Without feeling that I've done you wrong…

Still waters run deep
Shut eyes mimic sleep
Pursed lips hide pain
Flowing tears show shame…

Ay E, Ay E I O U and I don't know "Y"
Is it because you saw me laugh,
Then sigh?

9 stages of WombManHood

I'm unhappy living a lie
You can see what's in my eyes-
Is not in my heart-
And thus we chose to stay apart
Instead of together
To create misery & tears
Then sigh & cry
And finally fly
Off the handle
Each time we try to make it work
Life's too berserk…

Still waters run deep
Shut eyes mimic sleep
Pursed lips hide pain
Flowing tears show shame
Ay E, Ay E I O U and I don't know "Y"…?
~ 4/22/01 @ 8:30 AM to 9:05 AM

21st Century Freak

Yes! Yes! Y'all! The girl was a freak!
But not a freak of nature-
Nah a *freak of defeat*
She performed dangerous tricks
& *magnanimous feats*
Privately, *behind closed doors, or*
Publicly, in the street
"Get your freak on! Get your freak on!"
"Get your freak on! Get your freak on!"
The boys would chant
& the girls would chime!
Unconcerned she would oblige
And shake her booty to the rhyme in time
The girl was a self-claimed freak
She wore the title with much pride
And bore the look through rain or heat
She was a freak
Not the circus kind
Who covered their forms in shame
Nor the "old school freak"-
That Rick James freak
Who did, *but hid,* their freaky thang
She was a new age freak-
A sleek, black, *blonde-haired freak*
An over-weaved, blue contact wearin' freak
A sheikh-carryin'

Sunday morning *God-fearing freak*
Which was the only day she wore a skirt
Below her waist & buttoned her shirt-
Since he said *"cum as you are"*
And she came in his name-
Thank you Jesus!!-
And left with the name of others
Who would soon see her shame
When the sun set
For he,
Who she said,
Died- *for her sins*
Washed away her sins in his blood
A true flood-
For the sins she performed
Each night
Unabashed, unwashed sins
But she was
"Healed! In the name of Jesus!"
"Freed! In the name of Jesus!"
& washed whiter than snow
Each Sunday morning
Then clothed in filthy rags
By the night's first evening glow…
But how was she to know?
Who would tell her she was wrong?
She wasn't paid to be a freak-
It was the norm-
Black Entertainment (?) videos

Told her it was right
And that's where she sat each evening
Glued to music
That was oh, so tight!
She dressed as they dressed
And memorized each song
Then threw away her "daisy dukes"
And dressed up in a "thong"
She called her "man of the week"
And made a point to see
If he was up to *bling-bling it*
Since what she had, *"weren't free"*
Yes, a true freak of the week was paid
Though contagious she might be
And like a freak
She laid
Unprotected
So he could see
That she trusted him
Had lust for him
Was just for him-
For that night of sin-
And when he felt the need
To "bling-bling" it again…
But her freak got busted
By a lover she trusted
Whose name she could not recall-
And by the time she found out
The truth had come out

9 stages of WombManHood

Since she caused many brothas to fall-
They weren't tough like her
She stuck it out
While some of them *still stuck it in*
Hidin'
Spreadin' dis-eases & lies
Through spiteful,
Deadly
Venom-
AIDS got the freaks
To come out at night
But caused her to stay in
Yes ya'll! the girl was a self-named freak
Who lived to freak
Tried to freak
And then-
Died.
~ 6/29/01 @ 9PM

Thong Songs

It's another
Thong-thong-thong-thong-thong song
To you
But it's a setback in the countless efforts
Of unsung heroes martyred
& Raped
For the very thing
Of which you sing.
Some sistas are sitting back
Enhancing their behinds
And forgetting to *enhance their minds*
There's a *booty call* on the horizon
& too many lives will be taken
Since we spend time *pajama-jamming*
& not book-slamming
I'm fearing how far we will go
Before we decide to put back on some clothes
& cover our private memories
Indecencies now exposed
Since "*I got it to flaunt*"
The very words that haunt
My daughter's future existence
If vulgarities persistence
Does---not---cease…
I see you got your eye on another *pigeon* brotha
But without a smidgeon of sense

You won't know how to treat her
Since her womb
Is God's cocoon
& you're Godless-
Lawless-
Nah, *not flawless*
Marching on with your pants down…
How many licks will it take with my switch
To make you cover your tootsie roll?
Can't you see that you're the only one partying
At the party?
You dance with your eyes closed to this song of life
Is that why you got stabbed in the back with a knife?
Your woman has been taken for a prize
But when will you realize
That you have set the price?
You parade her as they paraded us on the block
But now
We shake our thang
And do "the walk"
A virtuous woman is a blessing to her man
She gives him strength to take a stand
As one in a million men marching
To reclaim our family's name
So ask yourself this:
"Are you willing to remain
Claimed booty with no fame
Singing Thong Songs?"
~ 10/2/00

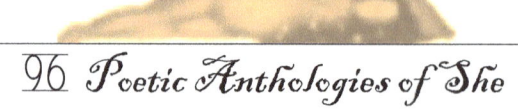

9 stages of WombManHood

She looked in the mirror plenty o' times, but,
today was the first time she saw herself...
"They told her to take a good look at herself.
She didn't know what to look for."

If I could fly…

If I could fly
I'd spread my wings past the pale blue sky
Past the confines of this universe
And only soar when I hit the black abyss
Beyond my thought's third eye…
Some bird I'd be
A shape undefined,
Unpronounced,
Undenied,
Free, to be
Me, myself & I
In the depth of the dark
I would kiss the sun-"goodbye!"
Until the coolness forced me to give it one last try…
Soar high…
Soar high…
Soar & fly!
Would be the meditational, medicinal beat of my heart,
I'd listen
Then in a trance I would fulfill all of its desires
Then beat my wings until I no longer needed them
And the gravitational pull of the earth-
My playground-
Would bid me to settle down
Then I'd plummet like a torpedo
Searching for a mark

Through the Universal dark
Past the burning desire of the sun,
Then ignite into a flame
As I hit the force field of earth's pain
The droplets of the clouds
Would cause me to smolder
As the smoke from my frame
Would beg to return to the *freedom of the black*
The tears I weep would evaporate,
Then condense into rain
Then I'd remember once again
How shallow it feels
To be embraced,
And encased on one planet…
Then one day
When I'm lying on my back bent weakened frame
I'd spread my minds wings in flight
And fly again...
~ 1997

100 *Poetic Anthologies of She*

Changes

Here she lies
In her own blood
Screaming for mercy
Begging for forgiveness
Hoping
Scoping
Coping
Choking
On old sweet-salt tears
Of fears
From years
And years
Then with old ears
She hears
A whimpering
Soft
Quiet
Purring
Like a cat
Cooing
Sweetly
Petite little whimpers
Gentle murmurs…
And then its over.
The pain is replaced
By more tears

And more fears
And then reluctance
For now
She is no longer alone
Nor will ever be
For she…
She is a Mother.
~ 12/30/00 @ 5:24:38 PM to 5:29:38 PM

God, is this Really Me?

Warm droplets from a sun shower beat freedom in my ears
The soothing wind from a cool rain
Caresses a smile from within
Then I think to myself
That I am indeed a *liberated woman*
Free from the ideals of this world
Free from the sexism
Racism
Materialism
And any ism & schism that binds
My black skin in
I rip off my earth bound form & rise
Into clouds that guide
Me slowly into a tranquil state
The higher I float
Is the faster I spin
Until 360 degrees
Become 360 degrees again…
And again…
And again…
This is amazing!
This journey I'm taking!
I'm smiling
In the midst of shame
I'm commanding
Myself

Yes, this old frame
I'm happy
It's my *fearlessness* they see-
God, Is this really me?
Unaware of boundaries
I dance within
Yet with no style
Who cares who sees?
I'll dance a while
Then fall asleep
And dance again
Because I'm free to be myself
The Universe is watching
God, is this really me?
 ~ 4/99-6/11/00

Summer Breeze

Summer breeze
With a wisp of your love
Touching me
Oh so near
Peaceful, like the wings of a dove
And then there was the pain
Calling your name in vain
Red roses lost their smell
White, at my feet would dwell
Peaceful, like the wings of a dove
~Summer 1980's

Raw & UnKind

Raw & unkind
Is what you seem to be
Raw & unkind
Malice smiling so sweetly
You told me that
It was a favor done for me
You told me that
Lies make love stronger
Than un-creamed coffee…
What goes around
Comes around
Sooner or later
What you deserve
Will be applied
To you in the end
Where the road is most rugged
Don't expect to survive
What goes around
Comes around
To the raw & unkind…
~ Late 80's

Violent Flow

I made it unbearable for you to live with yourself.
I am a mirror of your thoughts.
Your mind ain't playin' tricks on ya
When you look at me and see
The reflection of your desires
Imprinted around my eyes
In swollen pockets of blood
Deep red mud
Bruises my skin
From where you held me too hard
To make me stop talkin'
For fear that I would strip away
Whatever smidgeon of manhood you got left.
Don't forget that *men don't hit ladies-*
Oh yeah-
I forgot-
I'm a "bitch"
So that makes it all right
For you to "dog" me out;
Since I'm nothing but a "cow"
Which means that I got to take more of your "bull"
& God knows you are full of that!
In fact
If I hadn't fallen for you then
Maybe it wouldn't be
So hard for me

To get up now
And Stand.
~ 10/31/00

Betrothal (Betrayal)

She walks it alone
She walks down
The aisle
In a white gown
Stained with mockery
And laughter
For all present
Know
That she is
Far from untouched
As her stomach
Points
To three
More months
Before that rounded
Ball beneath her gown
Will drop down
Through her thighs
And reveal
To knowing eyes
An infant
Of countless lies
Told from
The mouths of
Her mother
Her father

Herself
And, her brothers…
To be
For they
All could not see
That by forcing
This upon her
And him
They were only
Causing more hell
Than heaven
In her life
But it was
Their selfishness
That forced them
To change
Into beasts
Of shame
And force
Her name
To be
Changed
To his
So now
Although she walked
Down the aisle alone
And endured
Years of shame
And pain

To no ones gain
She now has to sit
In a home
With a "SOLD" sign
On the door
With bags packed
On the floor
Two children
And, no more…
Now
Once again
To walk it
Alone.
~ 12/30/00 5:45:58 PM to 5:57:34 PM

9 stages of WombManHood

Growin' Pains

How do you know when you have gotten one year older?
Is it when you look around & see that your life has been
Spent & wasted on other peoples' dreams?
Is it when you look in the mirror & see a wrinkle in the cheek of your butt
Or feel it in your heart?
Do you forget very important things-
Like your age?
Your weight?
Or the fact that you've been married for far too long
To be feeling like you wish you weren't.
Does it come to mind when younger men want you as a lover
And older women want you as a friend?
Maybe you realize it when you tie your tubes-
Or wished you hadn't-
Want *one child* as opposed *to four*
Catch your mind wandering on an old love
Or your first love-
Or was it your last?
All your grandparents are resting in peace
And your parents look like your grandparents…
Or your husband's making comments about how "hot & fresh"
The young girls are-
And your waistline looks like a relative of the *baobob tree…*
If you haven't changed one negative thought into a positive
Or checked off another goal on your list of "things to do"
Then you may be older in age but lacking in wisdom…

Make this a year when you grow up!
Happy Birthday!
~ 8/7/00@11:30PM
a note to myself & the wise…

Mirror

They say Stella got her groove back
I'm laughin' at that
Because I'm lacking the fact within myself.

Then I look at you
And you seem to me
To be kickin' it free
At each party we attend
Old hearts that broke don't mend
But you claim he's "just a friend"
And that's *okay…*

Myself
My morals & my family
Would cringe if they knew
I was hangin' with you
Because you're spreadin' your love
in all the wrong places
You're looking in eyes of many faces
And submitting yourself *to a whore's life*
Committing yourself to a fool's strife
it's just damn degrading if you think about it

You watch each movie without looking within
You see the façade and ignore the grim
I'm surprised that you're learning at all
Since you keep interrupting to go chat with *Paul*

Or is it Ben?
Mike?
Or Kwame?
I'm confused
'Cuz your spreadin' the news
that *you livin'*
Did you mention the fact that in their beds *you're givin'* it up?
But not to God
To the god in Man
I know…
I know-
"He's just a friend."

Did you search your heart for love last nite?
Did you find yourself between his sheets?
I explored thoughts I had forgot
Ideas that died on subconscious streets
My meditative mind embraced
The intensity of my own face
Then took me back into a room
Shaped like a womb
My mother's
The depth of triple darkness soothed me
The amniotic fluid smoothed my skin
I floated buoyant in the warmth of my mind's eye
Then you came home
Picked up the phone
And called some guy

9 stages of WombManHood

You broke my thoughts to then relate
Some escapade of lust
Your fate it seems
Is based on dreams
That only you can see
It looks to me, *your life's a nightmare…*

How long do you expect to live remembering their names?
When do you think that you will stop playing these *childish games?*
I invite you time and again to join with me in prayer
I showed you strength within yourself
But I know you don't hear
Sis, I'm afraid that in our journey
You can't walk this road
Sister, I'm tired of having to carry
You and your extra load
I do believe we must accept to make the walk alone
It seems to me
You expect to make it on his throne
Or is that what he calls his ride-
I know- *you lied*
You're not his Queen
He's not your king
You both are just *doin' your thing*
But, you're the one who pays the price
They rob your days & steal your nites…

You're mixing blood within your womb
They're tearing apart your cocoon

You're virgin only by name-
I know…
I know-
"He's just a friend"

Guess how Stella got her groove back?
Because she started to live
Looking back on it now
That's when she started to give herself some time
Please open your ears & open your mind!

Looking past all the sexual emotion
And escapades of devotion
I see the reality of being free
But I don't need to fly to Jamaica to discover that fact
I can search my own heart
And get my "groove" back!

Think about that the next time you feel torn
Then pick up the phone in search of a warm space-
Outside of your mind
If you seek
You'll find
The liberty attached to self
It's the power that comes from nobody else
One day I hope you'll see the light
and spend time
with yourself
at nite.

~ 04/99

Old Stories

There's an ancient tale
They used to tell the children
About *going to hell*
But now they've changed
The tale to a fact
That hell lies within our state of mind.

No time to explain
Excuses are lame
As to why each and every one
Of us can't rise to the occasion
And free ourselves
And be
What the Creator wants us to be!

No matter what name you call him
You see the earth is in havoc
Death is a padlock
To the new beginnings in the cycles of life
360 degrees of life
Encircling our brains to a successful beginning
And a detrimental end
If we depend
On *following the followers*
And not *leading the leaders*

Your gift
Is your command of your ship-
Your body-
Your temple
Is the only true place of rest
It is best
To treat it holy
Solely
Because you have no other
And like your father
And mother
This too shall pass!
So get up and express yourself
To the last breath
And flow free as water
Purifying yourself
With prayer & silt
That's dust or earth
So we can become One
And stand as righteous
Before The One
And stop telling tales or fibs about hell
And live!~
To be nothing more
Than our greatest potential!
~ 12/2/99

Phoënix

Antediluvian Khemetian mythology
Taught me to be- The Phoenix
The Phoenix is free,
Self-combusting energy
That erupts into a flame,
Disintegrates,
Then rises renewed
Out of its ashes-
Yet arises not the same.
As a Phoenix,
I fly above self-hatred
Then see the productivity
Of the beauty within me
The lips I used to shun
Are *sensuous, velvet pillows of joy-*
Dedicated strictly to praise The One-
My breasts,
The mammaries I used to feed my son
Are temple oranges
Sweet upon my chest
The curves I used to show to please
Are shielded by fabric,
Silken,
Below the knees
I walk the walk of Ancient Trust
Not the old of harlot's lust

And with those that I associate
There is much love-
No hate
The Phoenix within
Destroyed the past
The form remaining is far from last
At night I retire my old skin
Then arise at daybreak renewed again…
Be a Phoenix~
Rise!~
~ 7/2/99 @ 2:00PM

Wake Up!

Oh Sista you're so cool,
Even with that damn cigarette you're making brothas drool,
You're so cool…
Cool…
Cool…
Cool…

Oh Brotha, you're so fine,
Selling drugs got ya ass doin' time,
You're so fine…
Fine…
Fine…
Fine…

Oh Mama, you're so bad
All the neighborhood men done broke your bed,
You're so bad…
Bad…
Bad…
Bad…

Oh Papa, you're so hype
Your son watched you beat his mama just the other nite,
You're so hype…
Hype…

Hype…
Hype…

You're so cool…
You're so fine…
You're so bad…
And you're just too damn hype…
But y'all have got to Wake up…
Wake up…
Wake up…
WAKE UP!!~
(Are they awake yet?!?!)
~ 6/19/96 @ 6:30PM

9 stages of WombManHood

Be True

Dost thou not see
That thou art a discouragement
To me?
"To thine own self be true,"
I thinkest
Then await truth's noble head to conquer you
But alas, I wait in vain
For in heaven's sweet name
Thine own heart bears the stain
Of neglect & disdain
I look deep into those *fearsome* eyes
And see no love
Just *despise*…

I look across the valley wide
As I entreat my form to prayer
If I should be able to pray
I know that *He would hear*
You creep as a serpent in the grass
Hoping to remain
Privy to my lonesome pleas
So strength you might maintain-
O'er me…
Canst thou not see
A greater force can read your thoughts?

Success lies not in numbers
But in faith
I ask for more
& patiently wait…
Your demise
Does not take too long
Three years don't pass before you're gone
I am quite tickled
As thou art forlorn
"To thine own self be true"
And that I surely now am-
Without you.
~ 7/02/01 @ 8AM

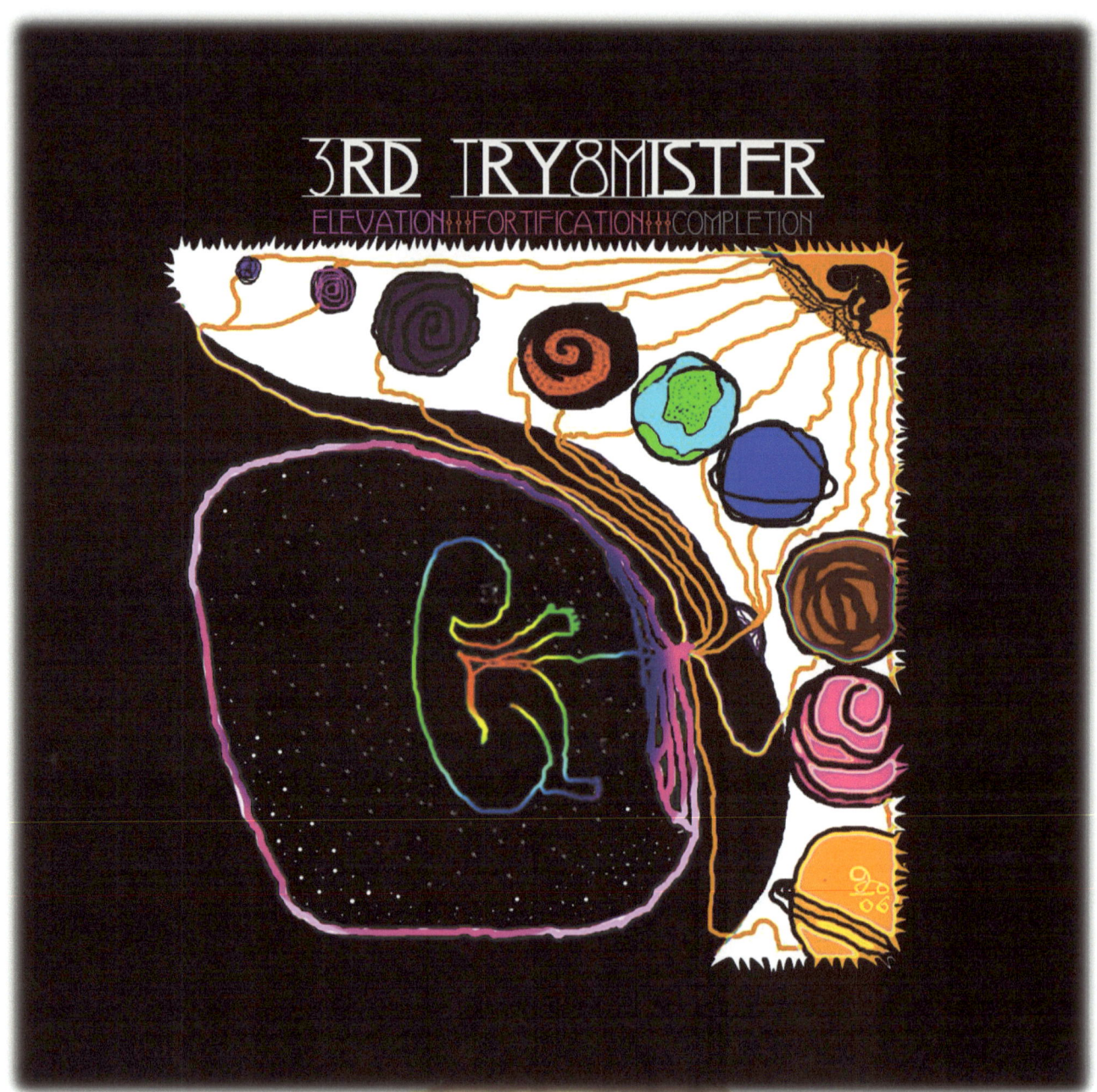

126 *Poetic Anthologies of She*

9 stages of WombManHood

She stood there praying, asking for guidance…

Then, it came.

"Self" she said,

"It has come to the point where I can no longer

Let you be who you think you are…"

Self Improvement

"Self" she said,
"It has come to the point where I can no longer
Let you be who you think you are...
You are going to have to be your *self*"
And so she cleaned up her *self*,
And made her *self* worthy of being her *self*
Then she cleaned up her home,
The filthy laundry was washed,
The beds- made
The trash under the bed- tossed
Into her Proverbial garbage can
And she smiled-
She smiled deep inside-
Her *self*
For she knew
That the struggle was over
She was free…
Now her paradise
Could finally begin.
~ 3/31/01 12:33:49 AM to 12:38:48 AM

Requiem to My Womb

I have exposed your innocence to guilt
I have allowed you to be used,
Relentlessly
For acts of low desires
And rough pleasures
My fantasy
Has been your nightmare-
My fleeting memories
Have shifted as the sands of time
But you have not forgotten
What has been so painfully carved
Into you as a chisel on stone…
Help me to remember
What I have put you through
So that I might beg your forgiveness
Oh womb!
You have nurtured my children
Four times
And released two full term
And two more before their time
Oh womb!
You have endured innumerable rapes
And felt my deep neglect
And hatred of you
Although you have been there with me
From the moment my first thoughts were conceived

And will be with me until the end
Of my physical conception of form
On this earth
Womb,
Help me to *heal you*
Of your ailments
Help me to *purge you*
Of any fibroids, cysts,
Dried blood, dis-eases & pain
I apologize for making you
A victim of myself
I seek your wisdom
As you have always been a womb
While I have remained a girl
And now have become a womb-man
You have helped me blossom into myself
Thank you for allowing me to use your space
For the conception of my greatest joys
Thank you for protecting me from myself
Since you have been consistently you
While I have not been myself
Thank you for enduring abuse
And allowing me to see that you were misused
Thank you for being my womb
And making me a womb-man
Lovingly yours,
Me.
~1999

My Lover Superstar

It was just as I'd dreamed
You and I, together, forever, *or so it seemed*
We would raise our happy family
Praying and staying
Together,
For eternity
So why am I feeling so bad
Could it be, Me?
Am I just goin' mad?
Why are you praying, *when you don't want to?*
 And why are you saying, *what I want you to?*
Are you feeling these things in your heart?
Or, saying these words so I won't depart?

Men come in all kinds today
Just like the burger,
You can have him "your way"
I don't care what others may say
To be my lover, superstar
My mind must be where you are
Make love to my mind, first
Teach me the secrets of the *Uni-verse*
As you fulfill this desire,
Allah will quench my thirst
Then heal the hollow,
of my heart.

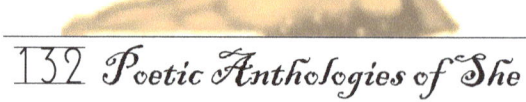

I want a man,
I don't *need one*
I need love,
But I want it to be true
There can be no attachments
If you're in love with me
For the one I love first is – *Allah*
Then the rest will follow…
Don't pretend to care about how I feel
Show me through your actions
Then my heart will know it's real
I'm too old for games
And too young to remain, *unhappy*
But mature enough to be committed
If you'll show me, love

Men come in all kinds today
Just like the burger,
You can have him "your way"
I don't care what other women may say
To be my lover superstar
My mind must be where you are
I'm not captivated by your body, good looks
Or your fancy car
If you entice my mind, and put God first
He will quench my thirst
And heal the hollow, (heal the hollow, heal the hollow)
of my heart…
~ 8/19/2006 10:07:52 AM

sing song

Her voice was too intoxicating to drink at once.
We had to take short sips and then find something
To *water it down*
So that the moist, chocolate-rich ether droplets would
Dissipate,
As we sat still long enough
To debate how much longer
We could sit on our hands
Before we were forced to kneel at the foot of the stage
Sit At her feet and beg her to
"Please… don't stop…"

The women in the room
Hated to let their men hear her sing
For it was she that would permeate
The rest of their nights
As they wrestled with men
Who called out her name
Without a care
In ecstasy
And without apology…

To herself and her own ears
She was doing her thing
Singing to the *countless vipers*
Who had poisoned her heart to love

Who had forced her to have to sing
In order to feed unspoken and unknown
Numbers of children
Some of those who really knew
Were not sure how to tell it
For they remembered it
Only when they were alone
Then forgot about it
When she entered the room
And started to drown their ears
With a voice of sundry tears
Or was it laughter?
For none could really tell if she were speaking to them
Or to someone else-
Perhaps a dear friend-
Or about a rumor that she'd heard
For she knew how to express the pain
Yet detached herself
From saying names

We *imbibed* her voice
We swished it around for longing hours
Hoping that we would be
The one
That she would sell her heart too
Then, just as suddenly as she began
She stopped
The music stopped
Then,

The longing stopped
For she
Was just
A singer.
~ 10/31/04 8:46 AM

A Day of Promise

They named that brown sugar coated baby *Promise*
For the day in which she was born
But her name proved to be more for her demise than for her success

She walked the burning gravel just like we walked it
But with a saunter of cool running water
Down a thirsting throat
As if life was nothing but a dance…

Her lips caught a beat
And her hips interpreted it
She heard with her feet
What the drums moaned into the earth
She kicked up long legs to allow the ground to move
And she captured sound with her ears…

This was Promise
You knew by her name that you would not be denied
And she could never say "no"
Since they named her for the day
In which she was born

"*I Promise…*" was her affirmation
Each day of each moon
As she shared what she owned in each room
If she chanced to disagree it was checked with

"But you promised me!…"
And she submitted to her signature of fame
In denigration's name

She failed to realize that in One was all her ties
And that her name was a declaration of success
Named to be *something,*
Someone,
Somewhere,
Somehow,
Some bull it seemed as
Some cow was calling her a "HO!"
Just out of her name they'd go
Before she promised them death
And kept that promise!~

"I *promise* I'll do better", he said
but back-hand smacked her anyway
Since she dared to talk about him like a dog

"I *promise* to be a better father"
He said as he slammed the door on
Her hopes and in their faces
Promises…
Promises…
Promises…
That's *Promise's* problem
Too many promises
And no *"word is bond"*

And *"bond is my life"*

Now she is a woman
Full of wounds with *salt in 'em*
Full of *bruises with bruises*
And sore legs
From *stretching her promise*
And *sharing her promise*
And *dancing with promise*
For no one of promise
Each night to feed *these children of Promise*
On promises!

She is a *woman of promise*
She was that brown sugar baby
They named *Promise*
But that they should have named "Queen"
Hey Y'all! This is Promise!
And she goin' do better!!
~ 12/3/1998

UnEntitled

refrain
Staring at my face through the window
watching the TiME pass me by
Wondering when i will ever know
what it feels like to fly
Manifesting nothing
Professing something
makes me feel more like a fool
Holding on to arms that make me feel charmed
But, they don't belong to you…

You let him pull you down.
You should have stopped him from the gitgo
But you really didn't know
That he would treat you like a "HO"

it's the beginning of the end
'Cuz when they dis' you- mis-use you
That's the same boyfriend
who will beat you
It's not okay for him- Treating you like trash
But you threw yourself at him- giving him that ass
Sold yourself to conquer sin
Gave up your God for Satan
What you've lost- you'll never win
As you were-

now, carry on...

refrain
Staring at my face through the window
watching the TiME pass me by
Wondering when i will ever know
what it feels like to fly
Manifesting nothing
Professing something
makes me feel more like a fool
Holding on to arms that make me feel charmed
But, they don't belong to you...

Woah Girl! Slow down-
now, here you go again
When will you take time
and let this cycle end?
Insanity is when
you keep doing the same thing
again
& again & again
and never change

refrain
Staring at my face through the window
watching the TiME pass me by
Wondering when i will ever know
what it feels like to fly
Manifesting nothing

9 stages of WombManHood

Professing something
makes me feel more like a fool
Holding on to arms that make me feel charmed
But, they don't belong to you…

Love.
Not worth your time with him.
Hate.
It's what you feel for him…
Rage.
At yourself for falling in love…
Sorrow…o..o..o…o
but, There's still tomorrow.

refrain
Staring at my face through the window
watching the TiME pass me by
Wondering when i will ever know
what it feels like to fly
Manifesting nothing
Professing something
makes me feel more like a fool
Holding on to arms that make me feel charmed
But, they don't belong to you…
They don't belong to you…
They don't belong to you…
So- now, I'm through…
~4/27/2013 @9:05 AM CST
© 2013 Tisa Muhammad

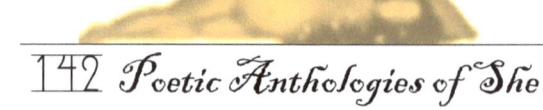

Pendant of Fools

I am a pendant on your chain of fools
But the rules I'm finding hard to understand
Since I'm yours…
And she's yours…
And yet you're *my man?*
I can't stand to see the snickers in their eyes
As I walk in on your arm
And they realize
That I'm just like all the women with *these guys-*
Yes, I'm a prize-
To be won
Used, abused & *stung*
Like the many women of *Rae Carruth*
I get used to the public attention
And then there's no mention of me
Since I was too blind to see
That *I was not being me*
But an animal in a cage
A monkey on stage
Juggling
Then smuggling a banana
That belongs to someone else
Getting broke off a small piece
That's dropped on the floor
Hungering for more
I leap for the door

And get bound in
To a contract of *sin & infidelities*
Abnormalities
That other women would dare not mention
If they had the intention
To do what I do and did for you
And men like you
Who come often and go
To lay with many more
Who are willing to store
Their love in a box
Or in socks
Filled with cash that they mash
Under wet feet
On a cold street
Trying to be discreet
On sleek corners
Like mourners
Their lace hides their face
And steals their heart
Each car that they meet
Makes them start to miss a beat
For the violence that they seek
Will soon be found
Be they stabbed or gunned down
No one will be around
Nor will they frown
When it gets to town
For *that's how the cycle starts*

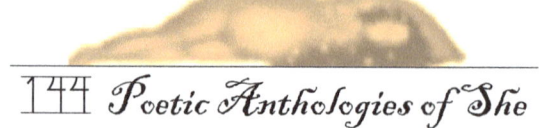

And ends
One moment
You're a stripper in college
The next-
A hooker with friends
And men
Too rich to spend more than a ten
So you can blow away his problems
With his wife
So he can get between your legs
And hide from life
And the strife that comes
As he comes
And goes as he flows
Into the church to renew his vows
And yet you sit
In a dingy room of your own doom
Waiting for the night to hide your face
Cancer gnaws on your womb
And numbs the space
What used to give you pleasure
Has no measure to the pain in your heart
Until you remember
The simplicities of its start-
In a kiss
With a man
So long ago-
That opened the sun in your eyes
And made your river flow

9 stages of WombManHood

Into an ocean of motion
At the time *so new*
That it coaxed you
To choose to be one of a few
On a link
In his chain
And there you remained
Maimed and stained
But then it was *cool,*
As you chose to be a pendant
On his chain of fools.
~ 01/01 @ 7:48-8:20AM

Wronged

Verse 1
I never knew a love like this could be
I never had a clue about you
Every open door seemed to be
Another way for me to embrace you
You opened dreams even closed eyes could see
but this was not our reality-

Refrain:
There was something in the way you looked
made me feel like, like an open book
It was something in the way you smiled
made me trust you, made me love you
but…. i was wronged….
so wrong, so wrong,
so damn wrong

Verse 2
If i had a chance to tell you this
I think that you would feel you conquered this
You made me feel as if i was the One
But then I realized that she was too…
Believed in you & every thing you said
What was the point of filling up my head?

Refrain:
There was something in the way you looked
made me feel like, like an open book
It was something in the way you smiled
made me trust you, i loved you~!
but…. i was wronged….

Verse 3
Hey! I'm talking to you~
Don't walk away until I'm through~
If you wanted to, you could have been for me
But now I know we'll never be!
Dedicated many nights to tears
Obsessed my pillow with nightmares!
Gave away my dreams of two, Gave away my dreams of you
I suffer in silence without you…!

Refrain
There was Something in the way you looked
made me feel like, like an open book, baby
It was something in the way you smiled
made me trust you, made me love you
i was wronged….
(Pause) Sigh…

Verse 4
I can't exhale living in hell
Until i rise and heal inside

No other way around this pain, but through it…

Extro
Something in the way you looked
made me feel like, like an open book, baby
It was something in the way you smiled
made me trust you, made me love you
Something in the way you looked
made me feel like, like an open book,
It was something...
~4/13/2013 @ 1:35 AM EST
© 2013 Tisa Muhammad

The Mask

Today I peeled the mask of the beast
Off my face and *faced the East.*

Today I removed the blush, the rouge, the flush,
Off my skin and *faced the Mosque.*

My eyes,
The liner Black, so dark-
No longer leaves its' Persian mark.

My lips,
No longer red & bright-
To corrupt my every thought at night,
With dreams of kissing my blackened prince,
Leaving crimson insignias upon his chin
Red's so unnatural on the skin
Unless it's blood.

I wiped away the grease, the stains,
Then faced the mirror with great pains…
"I'm beautiful,"
I whisper, deep in shock,
No longer hidden beneath the smock,
"Feigned beauty, curse you!"
I rage,
"Beast of beauty, shame you!"

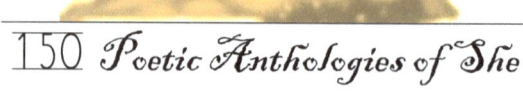

I scream,
Staring entranced upon the face that belongs in a dream.
Good thing I've moved that cloud of dust to reveal you to me.
To think, I've hidden all these years such divine in beauty.

Spread your tale!
Sing your tune!
Gaze, amazed at me!
Get drunk!
Get high!
Get wasted nigh,'
Entrapped in jealousy!
These are the eyes-
Brown-
You shall seek!

This,
The nose
Of which they speak!

The lips are full
The hair of wool-
Knitted in-
Joined to a peak!

The ears,
They hear your every word,
Of love,
Of lust,

Of hate,
They even hear the tempest rage
As death becomes your fate!

Die! Image of old beauty!
Be gone! Image of late!
My people seek to destroy the beast,
Peel off their masks
And seek the standards
Of the East.
~ 1995/199

Ain't that Something

verse 1
It was something that i had to see that day
to know i had no intention
to play with your heart & i made a brand new start...

verse 2
I know something happened when i
stared into your eyes and I knew
that you had that look~
and if i wasn't careful
I'd never walk through that door the same

verse 3
You know something was in your words
when you said that you and i could be
And i know you weren't lyin'
because you looked so true to me...

verse 4
It was something how you could feel
the way i felt and could comfort me
when i explained how much i was hurting
and why, and i felt like i could fly...

verse 5
Then Something convinced me

you and i could really be the manifestation
 of what I dreamed for years
and I could finally release all these tears...

verse 6

Then one dreary day something happened
when i stopped by to check on you
i noticed that you had company
and she was staring so damn hard at me...

verse 7

She had something in her eyes
that made me realize, I saw she was mesmerized
And I know that don't happen but one way,
& then one day

verse 8

Something was tryna convince me
that i was cra-a-zy when i started to
feel as if you were doing something,
something...

verse 9

something, was makin
me feel that this thing could be real and
i was in need of prayers~ so i,
i cried me a river...

verse 10

Then folks started telling me something
And that was really something
Because i didn't never feel
as if i couldn't trust you
Didn't you feel that way too?

verse 11

Then something in the way
that you loved me
Started to cha-ee-a-ee-ange
And then I knew that you were through
that damn near broke my heart

verse 12

Then something made me know
I was not acceptable
because U & I didn't fit and I
felt like a fool, a plumb fool…

verse 13

Then something clicked and the lights
went on and I was finally in the know
and if i sat there long enough
it might have seemed possible

verse 14

Then something told me to love myself
and release all this hate

And i know that i don't really want you..
Now, aint that something?!
~Saturday April 13, 2013 @11:48pm EST
© Tisa Muhammad

Inner Peace

There's no peace
like the inner peace
I feel in the Divine
When i close my eyes...
I'm floating

You carry me away to freedom
and like a dove i rise
through clouds i soar
above the physical confines...
then spread my wings in flight.

I drift on currents
that gently shield me from the pain,
the present- presents to my weak frame
I'm strengthened by your promise
that no weapon shall prevail
then through the storms i sail...

Unafraid of the terror ahead
Unaware that the danger around me,
surrounds me
As your cocoon gives me a web
of confidence...

In you i close my eyes

i meditate & bow
in obedience to you...
the Divine.
~ 1999

Free to be ~the handmaiden's journey~

Her silhouette reflected dark against the glass of the lake
She outstretched her hands to the fading sun
Then turning with the earth
She began to dance
Her fingers snapped to a deaf beat
And her hands rolled with the crystal waves
She twirled in the rainbow of the sunset
Until she fell,
Out of breath- into grass
She lay with her eyes closed to the universe without,
Then delved into the wombniverse within
There she listened to the raspiness of her breath
Her life force- *her kundalini-*
As her lips tasted the coolness of the air
Her chest rose & fell
Her muscles tensed
Then relaxed
She was absorbed with her inner evolution
As the earth made its revolution
One thousand, thirty-seven & a third miles per hour
She was free
Free to be what ever Allah granted her to be
She reached into her tufts of locing hair
And pulled strands of it across her brow
Until the desire to nibble it went away
Then, she nibbled her hair anyhow

What would the others think if they saw me now?
She thought
Then laughed at the notion
They chose to remain slaves to the system
She wanted to master this universe-
Not serve it!
The moon watched her encased in the grass
Until she drifted off into a deep sleep
Her dreams welcomed her for the first time
She smiled as they replayed the journey of her escape
Never again would she to be recaptured
By such hate & ill fate
Yes, this time she was free.
Not liberated or emancipated…
Free to be…
Herself.
~ 8/24/99 @ 11:50 PM EST

The fungus among us

There's a fungus among us
And I'm afraid its gonna spread
Once black people get freedom in their head!
They might just get these *highfalutin*[6] ideas
To climb on the balcony &
Stop standing on the stairs
Some might even think to step out on their own-
Stop paying Caesar & flick off the throne
Then there are the few who might decide to stay a slave
For a year, month, week or even a day-
And don't forget that revolutionary
Who lacks the *common sense*
That *not owning a gun*
Is true self defense
Don't fail to overlook the sistas with fake hair
Hiding a *natural* under there
Watch that brotha with the blue eyes
Who'll soon realize
That it's going around town
That *the Brown sees the lies*
Your mother & father who scar knees for peace
Might just be the first

---

[6] Highfalutin definition: adj. seeming or trying to seem great or important; pretentious, fancy; expressed in or marked by the use of high-flown bombastic language: pompous. First known use: 1839.

9 stages of WombManHood

To grab a weapon to this beast
That half naked sista clothed in a thong
Will soon realize
That her man done her wrong
These college educated
Might use their degrees
To help light the kindling
So the B.S. can cease
Yes! There's a fungus among us
That's sure gonna spread
Once we plant seeds of freedom
In our heads
All that we need is the joining of breath
Spoken in a word
We best soon not forget
….UNITY! *(blow)*
~ 2/22/01 6:40-7:15 PM

Revolution

An idea that I achieve through a dream…
A short dream that becomes a vision.
For a dream is unattainable, but a vision is beyond seeing…
It is believing!

When I choose to change,
I've revolved from old thinking to new.
When I refuse to accept,
that is when I have revolved into the new.

It is absurd to ask me to turn the other cheek-
I only have four, so what happens next?
Am I to start at the beginning, or do I get you from the start?
If I hit you back, I have revolved into a greater, thinking creature-
For a dog allows nothing to bite it, and a cat scratches its attacker-
So why can't I?

Revolution is an idea.

I thought it…
And it was.
I breathed it…
And it gave me life.
The whole thought of controlling my own destiny…
Gave me peace.

A woman who is beaten for fifteen years of a broken marriage,
Is empowered by the thought of revolting!
A man who is savagely dehumanized all of his earthly existence,
Is calmed by the mention of the name…

Revolution. Revolution. Revolution…

If I say it three times, will it change my existence?
If I teach my children about it, will it give them hope?
If I whisper it in your ear,
will you turn me in to the authorities who fear the very thought of such banter?
Or,
Will you join me?
Me and mine...
Me, mine and yours…?

We will be responsible for it one day.
If we plant the right seeds,
Then maybe we won't just be "emancipated"
Maybe we will be… "Free"!

Freedom. Revolution.

Revolution. Freedom.

Revolution is an idea.

A Revolution will be a Change…
~1996

The Heart of the Wombniverse

The heart beats throughout the whole wombniverse…

Tum-tump…tum-tump… tum-tump…

It pulsates through veins
Through organs
Throughout each organism
As like a steady unsung song…

Tum-tump…tum-tump… tum-tump…

It vibrates through the hot, molten core-
The heart of the earth-
It reverberates and shifts
Through ice of the earth's poles
It never stops its steady beat of life…

Tum-tump… tum-tump… tum-tump…

The macro-organism is reflected
In the only other womb
That twins the life force
Of the wombniverse-
The micro-organism called "womb-man"
And other warm blooded womb carriers
Who operate their bodies & bring

Forth their young after full term…

Tum-tump… tum-tump…

The heart beat is found
In the pulsating heat of the sun
And the reflection of the moon
Each planet must rotate
With the encouragement of this pulse…

Tum-tump…tum-tump… tum-tump…

The beat is orgasmic
As we too pulsate at orgasm
Or dance in a frenzy
Or meditate in peace
There still lies that steady beat…

Tum-tump…tum-tump… tum-tump…

Although our hearts
May cease one day
To duplicate this song
The life of our minds
Never ceases to rhythmically
Copy the beat
As we pulse with the earth
In our sleep…
Formless as wind

Yet still energy
We vibrate until we can whisper
The sound of the heart
In our mother's womb again…
And again…
And forever…

Tum-tump…tum-tump… tum-tump…
…fades out…
~ 11/26/00 In the AM

8th Stage
36 Weeks: E(x)ternal Chaos, Internal Growth

168 Poetic Anthologies of She

She must bring forth herself,

Wholly, solely,

Yet, so many say she can't...

"Womb, I have allowed many

to tamper with your innocence."

Unity (a Narrative)

I saw her every morning,
Sitting on the same corner,
Beyond our scornful, critical eye she sat,
Wrapped in tattered laundry from a yesteryear's fashion-
Worn out she was.
She tried to keep clean-she did-
Removing the excess dust from her garment
Rolling the dirt from her legs,
Arms, her breasts…

One morning I chanced to see her bathe,
Discreetly encased in a red blanket,
Removing each piece of her inheritance,
Scooping green water over her head,
Through untamed locks,
Across a dingy brow,
Under a calloused foot-
Purifying herself as if she were the Goddess Isis-
Yet she was a sister of the streets…
I watched her cleanse her *holey* shorts
Her ripped shirt
And grey underwear
In a corner pipe-
Using a sudsing agent
That could have been "Tide" or "Cheer"-
Had she had the tithe or good cheer

To purchase such
But more possibly it was from the hand cleanser
Located in the basement bathroom of *Sears*

Now it was night.
The dawn had set
And the sun that had nestled her
Into her daily duties of survival
Had dropped to allow the moon to take a bow-
She is sitting on the corner now-
Alone.
Had she been a man,
She could have worried less,
But she was *booty*
To the eye of the invaders,
And the freaks-
Who came out at night
Knew she was a woman.
They sensed her uncertainty,
Because I sensed it.
I watched her through my cloak of safety,
Because *I* had a home,
I had a bed
And *I* had a bus ticket
To board the first passing vehicle that took me to my immediate heaven.
Where would my sister turn?
What home did she have?
What bed would she lay on-
Without the fear of sharing it with a stranger?

And certainly,
What ticket did she have that would ensure her existence for tomorrow?
She couldn't bring herself to share her virtue
Even in that state
Yet, I was to sell mine,
At no greater cost than to acquire material gifts
And verbal compliments.
If I were to share her load
Would I too survive
And continue this same routine?
Or would I exchange my value for instant gain?
Would I sell the one thing I was instructed to keep?
Or would I guard it with such persistency, as she?
I knew that she was dreading the night
As much as I was welcoming it
I saw the night as a symbol of rest
Yet to her
The battle was about to begin.
Did she bet on life
As much as I bet on success?
Or did she just put her mustard seed of faith
In the one mystery she depended on?
But then again,
Did she even believe in a God?
After all, she must have prayed for bread
And received a notice of eviction.
Who's that girl?
I think.
Where did she come from?

And what drove her to that position…
Condition…
Eviction?

Did she even have a family?
Where were they?
And what stopped them
from guarding this Queen from a life of poverty?

We spend so much time bickering,
Arguing,
Fighting over foolishness,
When we should be building,
Constructing a good home-
Community-
Self.
We spend our time in opposition to others,
Not realizing we are opposing ourselves…
Why does my sister need to beg
When some of us our blessed?
We frown upon the act of selfishness
But are we in turn "selfless"
Or what we accuse others of being?
I point the finger of blame on you
But three fingers point at me.
Why don't we raise our babies to *look*
So that they can see?
I see my sister cloaked in dirt
And weep at my position

How can we learn to share our wealth
And save others from this condition?
UNITY.
~ 7/26/96 @ 8:58PM

Is it possible?

intro
Living LOUD in a quiet place
Can you see me?
Or, is it possible?

verse 1
Moving too slow in the fast lane
Makes you a victim to the Game
Folks don't even care to know your name
or give a damn 'bout what you sayin'
Some think that they can fool I
Use deceptive intelligence on We-
but, you bamboozling yourself,
and No one else~
Truth taste so good- to a belly full of lies~
so hurl it at falsehood 'til you destroy its mind
they say "if ye seek then ye shall find"
So don't you mind when you find out you're...

Living LOUD in a quiet place
Staring in the eyes without a face
Paying rent, but don't have a home
In a crowded room, yet all alone
When i cry, can you feel my pain?
Sun sets on me today,
So you'll rise up tomorrow-

But, will you know my name?
Is it possible?

verse 2
Thought travels 24 Billion miles a second
Sound travels 1, 120 feet in the same time
If we put more thought into what we said~
We wouldn't be afraid to speak our mind
If we stopped trying to fit in
Maybe, we could get to heaven
Let righteousness be your guide
& please don't let these fools ride~
As far as we know now,
We have one life to live
Will you let Fear be your god,
Or, will you fear God & Eat to Live?

Living LOUD in a quiet place
Staring in the eyes without a face
Paying rent, but don't have a home
In a crowded room, yet all alone
When i cry, can you feel my pain?
Sun sets on me today,
So you'll rise up tomorrow-
But, will you know my name?
Is it possible?
~Friday January 25th 2013 @5:33 AM EST
© 2013 Tisa Muhammad

La-La-Land Yankee

He wants to be a la-la land yankee
Living in the ill hills of Beverly
Sipping on champagne
Wearing someone's name
Trying to claim fame
Where there seems to be the flame
Of holy-wood Hollywood
Folly-wood
Where wealth has stood
For disgusting morals
Mistrusting mortals
Combusting portals
Infesting our minds
With this dream
Of living it up
Giving it up
While others starve
So you can drive
Your Mercedes Benz
Around bends
And be glad
That you're not sad
Anymore…
Because you finally
Made it through the door
Without having to work for

It…
Such *bullshit!*
Wake up!
The American dream
Is a *gotdamn* Nightmare!
Let the truth reign
Let the lies die!
And please God~
Please let black folk try
To love themselves
So we can fly
Free!
~ 8/12/2001@11:40:34 AM to 11:51:57 AM

It's a Dirty Shame

I got a call today black man
Somebody told me that you went & got yourself shot…
Allah loves not the aggressor.
Rumor has it that you were aggressive
And tried to eliminate another brother
Who eliminated you…
Not true?
Boo?
Then, whose fault was it then?
Word has it that *ya'll always tryin' to offend*
So I defend my son against the lies
Since you guys can't seem to
See that what you do affects me
My son & I can't stand by and have
His eyes cry after watching you fry
In the chair
Or waste away in the penitentiary-
When you don't have to be there.
Where did you learn to call our home a crib?
Some fib you told about being a man
When you can't keep a job and
Stand up for your black self.
I watch you *watchin' me*
And my baby girl-
Talkin' bout you gon'
rock my world!

Would that be with a gun?
'Cuz it seems to me to be your
First line of defense to the world's offense
Yet- *life's expense is on the fence*
Your suspense & mine
lies in who's going to die next…
It's a got-damn dirty shame!
~ 7/6/00

Look who's laughing now

refrain
You don't know what it feels like
Living your life on a dream
You'll only know what it feels like-
when you lose everything…

verse 1
Living life expecting everything to be the way you planned your whole life to be
Believing in something, someone- receiving nothing, yet expecting reciprocity
Opened doors
And Candlelight
Believing in love that's "oh so tight"
Sea salt scrubs that feel so damn right
Holding it down for you whenever you like
Teasing my pain- wasting time
Dreaming of kisses- sublime
Celebrating love that's so true
Only to find out the joke's on you

interlude
You saying much, but you ain't saying nothing
How would you like, to feel like I am feeling?
If you knew what its like, you won't go there
(Cuz you know that hurts me)
You don't know what its like so you throw
my love- you threw my love away…

refrain

You don't know what it feels like
Living your life on a dream?
You'll only know what it feels like-
when you lose everything…

interlude

You saying much, but you not saying nothing
How would you like, to feel like I am feeling?
If you knew what its like, you won't go there
Cuz you know that hurts me
You don't know what its like so you throw
my love, You threw my love away…

You don't know what its like-
or you won't keep this going…
You don't know what its like -
Here comes Karma- coming for you…

Baby you know what it feels like
Living your life on a dream
You finally know what it feels like-
because you've lost everything…

verse 2

You just standing outside my door, whoopin' and hollerin' 'bout you want more
Tryna beg me to come your way- fooled me once- twice? i don't play
Closed mouth don't get fed

Working hard to just keep my head
Living and breathing every word you said (memorized)
Babies need more than water & bread
Hustling hard to make ends meet
Hiding my love 'cuz I'm too discreet
"Got to make it"- my daily vow
Look who's laughing now?
~April 17, 2013 @ 11:52 pm EST
© Tisa Muhammad

Islam stole her daughter

You said last nite
That you don't want to be
A *Muslim*
Since they "stole" me
Yet in your presence
You have seen
Examples of Islam
That should be inspiring
To thee
But I think Beloved
The problem is
That you don't want
To submit
To do what Allah
Has promised you
And be
What He has yearned
For thee
So the next time
That you accuse Him
Of taking me from you
Realize
That to you
I have never belonged
Thus, you have never lost
What you have not owned

We do not own nor possess anyone
He does.
~ 8/13/2001 @ 6:28:26 AM to 6:33:45 AM

Know Thyself

verse 1
Did you ever have someone
try to tell you, that you were fake
and fraudulent too?
If you didn't know yourself,
you would surely believe,
if these snakes had their way~
We'd all be deceived
Know thyself
and Live in Truth
Don't be afraid
to Stand up for you

Swing that sword n' Cut that head
If it were left to them
We'd all be dead
Drown that lie in some truth
What Judas did to Jesus~
They doin' to you

refrain
We walk by sight and not by faith
that is why we can't elevate
Our brain was created in pure truth
So when you lie to me- you only Doin' you
If We Walked on water & kept our eyes on the prize

We'd get there sooner than we realize
Don't take credit, where no credit's due
Just be yourself, Baby, Do you…

verse 1
In every war that's fought- a soldier dies
Will you sell your rights for peace & save a life?
Are you here to rise or, here to fall?
Or, quite simply, here to compromise us all?
Your ignorance~ is Iblis
By the look on your face,
You ain't hearing this,
What Brutus did to Cesar ~
They doin' to you
While You dig a grave for me~
Go 'head & dig one for you~

refrain
We walk by sight and not by faith
that is why we can't elevate
Our brain was created in pure truth
So when you lie to me- you only Doin' you
If We Walked on water & kept our eyes on the prize
We'd get there sooner than we realize
Don't take credit, where no credit's due
Just be yourself, Baby, Do you…

We walk by sight and not by faith
that is why we can't elevate

Our brain was created in pure truth
So when you lie to me- you only Doin' you
What Adam did to Eve~
They doin' to you
What Brutus did to Caesar~
They doin' to you
What Judas did to Jesus~
They doin' that too…
So stop fooling yourself & Do you

~Saturday 13, 2013 @ 5:44 am EST
© Tisa Muhammad

I too, share your vision

I, too share your vision-
Of a world where hunger is only a memory
Satisfied by a horn of plenty
Where two or three are gathered in HIS name
And think one thought, dream one dream & feel the same…

I, too share your vision-
of One God-
Not separated by sects, dominations and one-way religions
But joined in unity in obedience under ONE banner called "TRUTH"…

I, too share your vision-
Of one people- differing in shades
But united in one language- LOVE
One people- who are not self-serving
Who don't bow down to nationalism, racism, sexism
Or any other impediment that binds them in-
But who stand up for the universal principles of
Freedom, Justice, Equality & Peace…

I, too share your vision-
Of a debt-free world
Where the only price you pay
And the only bill you owe- is LOVE
A world where bloodless wars are fought
Where differences are settled in PEACE

Where we "crack atoms" at dinner tables-
Elevating our minds to an eternal knowledge
And make pacts to "study war no more"…

I, too share your vision-
Of little black boys and little white girls walking together,
Hand in hand- through the hills of Tennessee
Standing atop Lookout Mountain
And seeing not a dream- that soon becomes a nightmare
Under an "inferiority-superiority" complex
But seeing our vision of ONE people
ONE world, under ONE God-
Who know themselves, Know each other
And know that our vision
Will soon be Our REALITY.
~ 02/28/02 (Dedicated to Auntie Lue)

She didn't think she could do it.

They knew she had no choice.

"Oh mama!~

What have we created?

Baby~ You created Yourself!"

So Grateful

refrain
i woke up this morning
staring at the sun from my window
feeling a love Supreme,
knowing that through you i would grow~
though we've had our ups & downs
i've learned many things that i'd never know
If it hadn't been for your sacrifice
in the honour that you gave me when you saved my life

verse 1
Well It's simple:
I'm feeling so grateful.
Now, that's a miracle,
coming from a life so painful
Your love unconditional
exposed emotions that were deep within my soul
you filled my cup tidibee til it overflowed
showed me my value through your righteous principles
Many may look at me & think that I'm so *cra-ee-zy*
None of them can pay me~ enough to even phase me
When you came in my life
Your presence removed all that strife
And now that I have changed this~
I've realized that I'm beautiful!~

9 stages of WombManHood

refrain:
i woke up this morning
staring at the sun from my window
feeling a love Supreme,
knowing that through you i would grow~
though we've had our ups & downs
i've learned many things that i'd never know
If it hadn't been for your sacrifice
in the honour that you gave me when you saved my life

No! Don't you Envy me~
'Cuz you don't know what I've been through
My life is no better than yours
worked my fingers to the bone~
Just say these words to you:
It's when the trials are rough~
you'll discover all the gifts buried inside of you
and it's at those moments
that you'll really learn to be thankful~
For the love Supreme
found everyday in a smile
For the kiss of a baby~
undeservedly~ yet so worthwhile,
For the arms that embrace;
words, that shelter you from the storm
For the prayers of your mother
lift you up when you fall down....

refrain:
i woke up this morning
staring at the sun from my window
feeling a love Supreme,
knowing that through you i would grow~
though we've had our ups & downs
i've learned many things that i'd never know
If it hadn't been for your sacrifice
i woke up this morning
staring at the sun from my window
feeling a love Supreme,
knowing that through you i would grow~
though we've had our ups & downs
i've learned many things that i'd never know
If it hadn't been for your sacrifice

~Saturday April 13, 2013 @9:55am EST
© Tisa Muhammad

Blessed

If your soul connects with my own
Does that mean that you're my soul mate?
If you speak into my heart
Should I grant you the smallest part
Or the section that you deserve?
Your words still ring clear to me
You spoke about this as a "meantime" thing
So in the mean time I sit here waiting
Contemplating the answers of my inner eye
To see the tears I cry & grant me peace
"Is this the one?" you asked
"Of Course!" I replied,
Since I can't see past this pain & look beyond the sky
I fear the unknown for known reasons
Make the tangible, intangible~
Quests~
I request~ to question
Then seek to find the answers in my mind
You said that I am a "beautiful, intelligent and much loved being"-
But seeing~ *is believing*
And believing~ *is receiving*
And receiving is…
So freeing!
I steal away to reclaim what is rightfully mine
I shield my ribs & protect my spine
As I climb back within my wömb

And find no room
For it is occupied by hatred & denials
Aborted hopes & trials
I scream in anger
Then curse under my breath
Since the solace that I seek
Is compact with regret
I fret over the time I take
To heal & cleanse my soul
Then think about advice you gave
To welcome new & release old
My womb cries for me-
As a river flows between my legs-
Then goes towards the earth
The only trace that I was there
Lies in the crimson grass
That is no longer "green" with envy-
But healing-
I regain feeling in my legs
And walk
Then run
Then fly!~
Past the sky
Into *large, black, awaiting arms*
Of unconditional universal love
I bathe myself in droplets of ether
Until each sacred inch of my nakedness
Is clothed in a golden light
That pierces deep into the night

Of ignorance
When I watched myself in a mirror
And hated what I saw-
"How do you see men?" you asked
"As trees" I replied,
Your spittle washed my third eye
Until I saw men as they are
And myself as I AM~
BLESSED!
~ 7/1/01 @ 6:20AM

Can You Feel it?

refrain
Can you feel the healing music?
The music in my soul
Can you feel it? Feel it? (2x)
The music makes me whole
Music makes me laugh-
Music makes me cry
Music makes me feel love, oh so deep inside!~

verse 1
The music lives in me
the Music makes me believe
that if i keep on giving my all- then i know i can achieve
the music makes me go
its the music that rocks my shows
Yes this music makes you feel in ways you didn't even know

refrain
Can you feel the healing music?
The music in my soul
Can you feel it? Feel it? (2x)
The music makes me whole
Music makes me laugh-
Music makes me cry
Music makes me feel love, oh so deep inside!~

The music lifts me up- when I'm feelin down-
Music soars my soul-
There's medicine in sound
Music freed the slaves
Taught them to Believe,
Do for Self & Rise
*Music's Supreme Wisdom, you see?

The music lives in me~!
The music lives in you!~
The music is a Universal Connection
of the Supreme Soul~!
~4/1/2013 @8:01 AM EST with Ashlynd Scott

200 Poetic Anthologies of She

Sacred Womb

The sacredness of my womb
My laboratory of room
Not wasted space or an empty spoon
That you dig out to your belly's delight
Or seek gluttonously at midnight
But a temple for which you should fight
Not hurt, tear, scorn or spite
But in which you should see the light

A sacred womb that extends life
Not a contentious space to make your strife
But extend life-
Your life…
My life…
Our life…
Of which you can't decipher
Or you would not despise her
Since she is your daughter
Mother
Girlfriend
Or wife
A womb that grows seeds
Sacredly…
Secretly…in triple darkness
For nine moons of time
Mystery known by design…

Mystery kept by Divine…
Mystery revealed in due time
But still a mystery…

A sacred cocoon of metamorphosis
Birthing golden butterflies from crystal silk
Sent on sacred journeys to the sun
Toasting wings soft as milk

A sacred labyrinth of safe space
A tantric passage on earth's face
Circular patterns of endless time
Encoded 19, 11 and nine
A velvet womb
To seek and find…Yourself.
~ 11/19/00

Sacred Warrior

Sacred warrior
Standing atop a mound
Larger than life!~
Massive magnificence in disguise
I close my eyes
Then inhale tight wafts of perfumed air
Through my lungs they soar
As I explore
The depth of a realm beyond my eyes
My physical eyes
As my third eye
Perched atop a crooked brow
Looks within and wonders how
My vessel had survived 'til now
Without consciously being aware
That I was starving for this air-
Of freedom-
I spread my arms 90 degrees
Then fall weightless upon my knees
Then as if without control
I start to sway
A river's roll
Rolling formlessness
Yearning *warmlessness*
Peaceful *stormlessness*
I am a dance

I am a trance
This is romance
That no one before me
Could see…
As I choose to lay still & BE…

I am a sacred warrior.
This is my sacred journey.
I have awaited my appointment
But now I am anointed
Now I stand upon a mound
As an eagle on a branch
And wait for the winds of freedom to take me
As they shall not forsake me
On my sacred journey to the sun.
~ 10/7/00

It's Morning (Wake Up!)

The sun rises in the east
And so do the heads in prayer
Amen Ra,
Allah,
Jehovah,
Jah,
The "All in All"
Is there

Frankincense burns & swirls
And kisses the sun
In recognition of a new day
Welcoming one who will come
And walk the earth
Trillions of years later
And trillions of years more to wait
Recreate
Reproduce & relate
As we perfect our perfection
In *His image*.

There's Myrrh
Her feminine essence is Isis
The moon is the night
She sizzles at noon in her own temple
Recognizing

That no nation rises any higher than its woman

As no sun is any higher than itself at noon

Heads swoon & swirl

As hair unfurls itself

And becomes braided with gold

Colored with pastes of henna,

Sandalwood, and ancient names unforgotten

Yet untold

Sweet sweat fragranced with musk

Is bitten before it bites

Purifying the temple it lays on

Washed away in the Nile

No denial as to the fact that this civilization is the oldest

Antedilivian pyramids boast of a landing site

Long before airplanes & space ships were invented

We wait

We see

We smell

We touch

We hear

Our hair encases our heads

It flows in dreads

Locked or open

The curls now mocked were beauty unspoken

We adorned it then

We mourn it now

Tap ourselves on the back and

Wake up…

Wake up…
WAKE UP!

Burn Frankincense & myrrh in celebration of yourselves!
Accept your own & be Yourself…
Yourself…
Yourself…
Your self…
~ 1997

The Time

There is a time for Love
There is a time for Peace
There is a time for War
And in that time there's time for more

There is a time for Warmth
There is a time for Cold
There is no time to waste
All things change as we are told

There is a time to rise
There is a time to fall
Do we not realize~
Now's the time to manifest all?

When will you choose to rise?
When will you realize?
Why do you choose to stay,
Living inside your fantasy?

It's time to move us forward
To change our destiny
We're no longer enslaved in chains,
We've been set free~
~9/11/2014 @ 12:18PM EST

Eye Want to...

Eye want to create with you—
Your beauty, unadulterated, enticing & oh, so mesmerizing
~ *encompasses me*~
steadily, thoroughly, absolutely stimulating my femininity

Your laughter tickles & pulls on my emotions, until,
thoroughly at your mercy I too submit to it as a smile escapes my lips

Your wise dome sits atop steady & firm shoulders as Atlas
~ *you support a world of wonders*~ so strong,
yet, oh so very, gentle,
you gently speak and say my name

You complete me. Yes, you truly complete me,
My twin, essence cannot match the fragrance
that wafts forth from your breath
& inspires me to breathe-

Breathe for life…
Breathe…

Breathe for Love…
Breathe…

Breathe~ *for healing*…
Breathe…

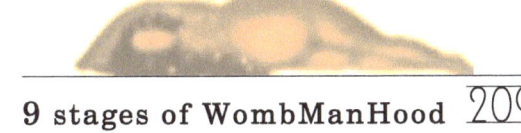

9 stages of WombManHood

Breathe~ *embrace this feeling…*
Breathe…

Ah yes, this breath of life is a long, cool sip of hydrogen bathed in oxygen
~ Water

Water that washes me…
Water…

Water that soothes me…
Water…

Water that embraces me…
Water…

Water that births me…
Water…
Water that satisfies my thirst-
 ~ 06/ 2012

Shë Journey (unfinished story)

It was unlike any other journey she had taken.
She chose to begin it on a beach.
She loved the water, rather, she adored it.
She never knew what it felt like to have it softly surround her feet, not that she could remember, since she was so used to city buses and filthy alleyways…

However, she knew that the sensation would be good.
The water- kind to her- allowed her to enjoy a refreshing walk on the sand with warm, salty water licking her toes and shallow waves inviting her to walk and immerse herself deeper into their glory…
~ 11/4/05 7:30 PM

The depth of her beauty would not be

If it were not for Him...

And if, for nothing else, for that,

He is to be Honored.

"When you takin' she back?"

"When you takin' she back?" he said,
"We're not, she's here to stay," said Mama,
"you will just have to learn to love her..."
And so, you did.

"When you takin' she back?" He said,
"We're not, she's here to stay," said Papa,
"You will just have to learn to love her..."
And so, you did.

"When is he comin' back?" I asked,
"He's not. He's there to stay," said Mama,
"You know that he had always loved you..."
And so, he did.
"When is he comin' back?" I asked,
"He's not. He's there to stay," said Papa,
"You know that he had always loved you..."
And so, he did.
"When are you comin' back?" I asked,
"I'm not, I'm here to stay," said Toussaint,
"Tis, you know I'll always love you..."
And so, you will...
~ 05/16/06

Dedicated to my beautiful, Beloved, Older brother, Toussaint who taught me what it really means to be loved, unconditionally... He was the manifestation of my guide, telling me that I would do ALL of this and more... I have come to see how RIGHT he really was... ASHE! This was written the morning that he last visited me to kiss me & tell me "I LOVE YOU Tisa..."

Poetic Anthologies of She

May Allah always bless me to NEVER betray such LOVE!
In Loving Memory of
Toussaint Donald Gabriel Farrell

His Sacred Sun arose: Sunday, December 27, 1970;
His Sacred Sun set: Sunday, May 14th, 2006 (Mother's Day)
                                    He was Sacredly Buried: Friday May 19th, 2006

Beautiful One

We searched the sky for signs of his beauty
The Earth whispered in our ears that he was near, and yet so very far…
When We felt compelled to ask,
We called Z to see if she could tell us where she left him last
"in the fields, under the golden rays of sun," she replied…

There We ran, where the golden rays caressed the Earth and kissed the sky
The flowers whispered in our ears that he was near, and yet so far…
When We felt obliged to ask,
We called Z to see if she could tell us where she left him last
"in the hills, under the spectrum of the rainbow," she replied…

There We ran, where the spectrum bathed the Earth and nestled the sky,
The rocks whispered that he was near, and yet so far…
When We felt required to ask,
We called Z to see if she could tell us where she left him last
"in the trees, under the shadow of the mountain," she replied…

There We ran, where the shadow draped the Earth and cloaked the sky,
The leaves whispered that he was near, and yet so far…
When We felt bound to ask,
We called Z to see if she could tell us where she left him last
"in a boat, under the soft glow of the moon," she replied…

There We ran, where the soft glow embraced the Earth and reflected the sky,
The waves whispered that he was near, and not so far…

So there We searched
And searched
Until We came across a stream of majestic light that flooded the entrance to a cave
Inside We crawled, careful not to disturb the delicate silken thread
Of a spiders' web

He lay, sleeping, carefully wrapped in swaddling blankets
And there, at his side, We sat, rocking him as he slept
The wind gently whispered in his ear that he was loved, so very dear…
We told him Z had left him here, that We alone could oversee his care
Then, he smiled, for now he knew that all the times he felt alone-
Abandoned, and unloved-
Although so far away we seemed,
Undeniably,
We were always there.
~ 3/13/2006 @ 7:00:55 PM

He was "Love"

He painted pictures with his mouth
Each word that deliciously rolled from his tongue,
Enticed their ears…
He spoke of beauty that their eyes had not seen,
Smells they had forgotten;
Feelings they could only imagine with their heart
He was a poet
To them he was an artist
A rare jewel laid in gold
An inscription in the Taj Mahal
He was love-
Incarnate love-
They tasted his love in his prose
His voice soothed them,
Encouraged them to imbibe his words
Intoxicated, they sat under him,
Lolling their eyes on him,
Hanging onto each phrase,
Lolli-gagging, waiting for him to finish
So that they could snap their fingers,
Clap their hands
Or rejoice!
For his voice
Had given them the push they needed
To, live…
To, exist…

To, Be.
He closed his eyes
Accepted their accolades
Bowed,
Shut his book
Then left them
Insulted,
That they had not been listening
Offended,
That they had mis-taken his words for a hoax
Over-looked his emotions
Used him for sport!
He resisted the notion
That they could possibly understand how he felt
How he was feeling
What he was feeling
He deemed them, unredeemable…
But, he was the one.
He was the culprit.
They enjoyed his words for what they were
He enjoyed his words for what they were not
He painted pictures with his tongue
But lacked the canvas in his mind
They saw,
What he failed to see
They felt ,
What he failed to feel
He fashioned emotions that he yearned into words
Simple words that lacked any direction

He soldered phrases
That seemed best left apart, when apart,
But were stunning when brought together
He was creative
He was an artist…
Unto himself
He was just a poet.
Of himself,
He was nothing.
To them…
He was love.
~ 8/26/2001 @ 10:04:20 AM to 10:36:26 AM

One

I am dazzled
Bewitched & frazzled
I think its love I feel
I wonder if it's real?
I lay awake-
Late-
Envisioning you making
Love
To me
In the most intricate way
I find it hard to see
How
We could delay
The process
If I were not possessed
Compressed
Or invested
With
Commitments
It would soon be
Enticing-
The idea, I mean-
Inviting-
Making love, I mean-
Uniting
Our family trees

To be
One.
~ 7/14/2001 @ 11:07:22 PM to 11:14:31 PM

222 *Poetic Anthologies of She*

Ebony

That was you just calling me
Your voice rang strong & true
Like chocolate hues of sweet ebony
You do a body good…
I should dedicate myself to you
Like any woman would
But I wonder how I'd feel
If you felt like I should…
I'm missing you
And that sweet caress
Those soft words
And kind smiles
I'm yearning for that manliness
Those hands
And lips
And styles
Of fashion that we share
Unique
Artistic miles
And miles
Of educated talk
That walk
Encouraged me to stalk
You every day
After school
And be your fool

You schooled me
On the way to be
Liberated,
Loved,
And free.
Like Ebony,
Wood.

~ 7/11/2001 @ 10:40 PM to 10:51 PM

🦋 *Dedicated to Lowell Wilson, aka "Sweet Ebony", my Beloved childhood sweetheart, brother, confidante & Friend for life! :o)*

The healer

These rough, large hands belong to a healer.
The fingers sit strong
On a well shaped palm
All five become ten
When the power is within…
You nurtured my wömb with those hands.
You found the center of my uni-verse
You kissed me, there
And whispered words of love, there
And stroked me, there…
Then, came all these tears
I released my pain into those hands
You are my gentle king.
You are my best friend.
You are my healer.
There is nothing that will block us now
From going together
And growing together
And knowing together
What we never knew
We now know
And will always
Until we meet our end-
Which will be the beginning
Of our union
Again

~ 11/29/00 9:10AM * *To Russell, in better times…*

Mine. (reclaimin' my own)

I'm envisionin' you now
Smilin' at me as we "pontificated" our feelings
Tryin' not to stare in each others eyes…
You were so fine, *yessuh!*-
But I dared not look beyond your chin-
For fear that I would wake up in a daze-happily-ever -after,
And, naked…
You shared with me your vision of a world so pure and true
It was as if I were speaking to myself
Looking at me in the form of a man
I was mesmerized by the endlessness of your wisdom
And the simplicity of your words
The ease of your tone
The beauty of your lips
And I knew at that one moment
Who you truly were…
Mine.
~ 10/23/2006 10:40:12 AM

And, Be.

Speak to me, beloved lover of mine,
I yearn to hear your voice
Delicately tickling my ears
Stimulating my olfactory for a whiff of what
You possess that lies beneath that cool exterior
Might I know your name?
No, not the one that you think belongs to you
The one that you were blessed to never know
Yet knew
Since you have lived up to it completely
Yes,
Beautiful
That is the name of which I speak
And as I say your name,
Know that I desire to feel the same
Betwixt thine legs
Alas, between thy knees is where I wish to lay my head
As I dream about you
Day in and out
And in and out might you enjoin
Thineself to mineself? *(smile!)*
As we dine and wine and inter-twine ourselves
In this eternal dance that some
Might think should be called "romance"
But that we simply call "sacred"
Perchance, you might decide to be

My lover for eternity
Or,
You might not
But, until then
Let's decide to remain more than friends
And laugh
And love
And live
And give
And,
Be.
~ 11/1/2006 1:25:22 PM

Ashé[7]

Today I felt the sun smile at me
As I lay beneath its gentle rays
An epiphany shone upon my face
And this word crystallized before my eyes-
Ashe
Yes, as it is, it has been, and always will-
Ashe
That best describes the feeling that you send
Through my kundalini, up my spine and into my head
Ashe, ashe
Oh yes, and It is so…
Ashe
Through your love, I am nourished and thus, I grow
Ashe, Ashe
Ah, yes!… I know
The first time that we agreed to be as one
And as was promised
So, it was done
Ashe
I can't help but realize
How much you have opened up my eyes
To happiness and a love, supreme
Ashe Ashe

---

[7] **Ashe** (pronounced Ash-AY) is a Yoruba word **meaning** power, command, and authority; it is the ability to make whatever one says happen. Often summarized as "so be it", "so it is", or "Be, and it is".

Beautiful one, you make me scream!
And rejoice!
As I hear that gentle voice
And sing your name
Ashe
Yes, it is one, all is the same
Ashe Ashe
You bring me peace
Ashe
Through you I reach to endless heights
Ashe Ashe
I now believe I can fly
Ashe
Speak words of wisdom in my ear
Ashe Ashe
Your truth washes away my fear…
Ashe Ashe
Ashe Ashe
Ashe Ashe Ashe…
Ah! So it is!
Thus,
It is So!
~ 11/2/2006 8:51:23 PM

The God in We

verse 1
T'was a very warm July
when i first laid eyes on you
I didn't even wonder why
the sky was so damn blue
Every face -
seemed to smile
The Earth stood still for a while
Yeah~I'm telling the TRUTH, baby!

Naw, i can't forget it-
 t'was all so copacetic
Everything that you promised
fed fire in our romance
Sunday morning -so boring
Until- that phone rings...
Decided to crown you King
And make me your Queen!~

refrain
It's the God, The God in Me~
that makes me comfort you!
It's the God, The God in You~
that elevates me too!
It's the God, The God in We~
that unites the two!

Yeah, I See the God that's in You, baby!

verse 2
You don't take me for granted
Brotha- Your love- i don't reject it~
Even if once in a while~
We quarrel, act dumb or like a child
I need you to know right now
That this love thang is real
So baby, How does it feel?
Let me know right now,
Do you want my love?
Do you want my heart?
Then baby- Keep The God on me
You cherish me
And I cherish you
So Baby- Keep the God on me
With God in between
This love will stay true
Ohh baby- Keep The God on me

Feels… oh so good~
Lovin' on you~
Your love's so true~
I See the God that's in You, baby!
~ Saturday April 13, 2013 @2:07am EST
© 2013 Tisa Muhammad

232 Poetic Anthologies of She

It's All Good

refrain
Oh allrightnow~
Baby, it's all good!
And it's DYNOMiTE
like we knew it would~

Oh *allrightnow~!*
I said, It's all good
Keep SHiNiN' YA LiGHT
like we knew you would~

verse 1
Docta, Docta?
What can you see?
I got a temperature
that's so Hot & Heavy
Can't move my head
or close my eyes
can't keep from smilin'
Am I still alive?

Can't get this man
straight out of my head
Can't seem to think-
maybe I'm dead
If it continues

Where would I be?
Oh, is this like eternity?

refrain
Oh allrightnow~
Baby, it's all good!
And it's DYNOMiTE
like we knew it would~

Oh *allrightnow~!*
I said, It's all good
Keep SHiNiN' YA LiGHT
like we knew you would~

verse 2
We're no Bonnie & Clyde
We Akhenaten & Nefertiti
'Cuz we rules with pride
like love is meant to be
We keeps it rolling
And our is love growin'
As long as we relate
this thing should precipitate

Clear skies ahead
Winds are calm & fair
Despite Atmospheric pressure-
We ain't goin' no where
Storms come & go

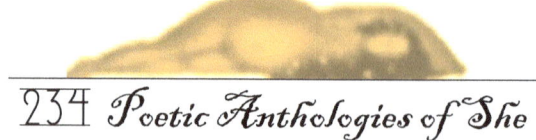

as we bond & grow
We'll soon know
If it stands the test of time-
so take no mind

refrain
Oh *allrightnow~*
Baby, it's all good!
And it's DYNOMiTE
like we knew it would~

Oh *allrightnow~!*
I said, It's all good
Keep SHiNiN' YA LiGHT
like we knew you would~

verse 3
Eenie, Meenie, Minnee Mo
You got this sista in ya tow
I don't care wherever ya go-
I'll be there~
i Ain't down with no competition
You up with me- then I'm the one
Saint or Sinner- Come get you some
Everlasting life in the land of Sun

No, Im not perfect
And neither are you
But If we stay in the light

We'll surely make it through~

I know we can't see
What dangers lurk ahead
But there's 196,940 thousand square miles~
Nuf said.
If we stay in tune,
allow our pineal glands to flow
We should sense the Time,
Stay in the know & let our Egos go...
~Saturday April 13, 2013 @ 1:40pm EST

One (Their Story)

…The Beginning…

She walked as quickly as her legs could carry her.

Almost breathless, she had the urgency to run, fly and skyrocket into the jet black ether of the *Wombniverse*, if only it could save her from the feeling that was overwhelming her femininity. Unlocking an essence of beauty, desire and sacredness that had been sheltered and hidden away for years.

"What manner of man is this?"

She asked anticipating an answer, knowing that she would not. Not in that way. She already knew what kind of man he was. She knew him because she *knew* him…

He was the Black God that embraced her in the *Temple of Tehuti* and inscribed his name into her heart, as he danced around her *nineteen times*! He was the King who traced his lineage through her womb and promised himself that he would spend trillions of lifetimes more with her, for only she could raise him to heights that no other woman, or man had done, before then. However, this too was entirely dependent on which life they lived together, for at times she was birthed in the form of the man, and he as a woman.

He was the one who sat down and taught her that the *breath of life* that exists in all living things, existed first in the Originator of the Universe, then was breathed into her, then into him…

Oh how she loved this man! Ah, how could she resist him? When she first laid eyes on him, love was the only option. He was the black pearl that so many searched for, and very few could attain. *So was she*. He was more precious to her than 50 fleets of airplanes, each one full of 1000 head of sheep. *So was she…*

She could not fathom Earth and her existence, before he was made manifest. *It was all good*. He made her smile. She didn't feel filthy around him, for to him, she was a diamond in the rough, anxiously awaiting the delicate hands of precision of one who would fashion each facet of her being, bringing forth her iridescence…

She would willingly submit to this man. He was invaluable to her, as he was the *music* in her song, the *ochre* in her painting, the *Sun* in her Sky, but above all of that he was hers.

9 stages of WombManHood

As to his beauty…? One could not bear witness to it alone, as one thousand already had, for he was good and she was pleased.

She pondered for awhile, wondering how could she best describe this Brother?

Mere words could not explain, as it was that feeling that remained when he looked at her, or smiled with teeth of ivory that brightly shone through velvet skin of iridescent melanin rich hues found only in the depths of the Earth's womb.

He was a prayer answered, period. She went through her entire life looking forward to their reunion. It came to the point that she almost forgot his face or the magnificence of his voice. Although they spent trillions of years with him in diverse dimensions of time, each life varied, as each time she saw him, he was transformed.

She remembered him as they wandered together through the hills of Tibet. Then, he was her childhood friend. She remembered him to be curious. It was delightful to see the light dance in his eyes every time he saw something that excited him! He was blessed with the gift of making it into a story or song~ drawing *lifelike* visions in their minds!

He tranquilized her then with fantasies of vast Kingdoms of queens with rich golden honeyed skins and fiery eyes or kings of gingery complexions with soul-searching charcoal eyes, all growing from the jasmine of his mind!~

She climbed into his mind's eye & nestled comfortably beside him there on raised silken cushions delicately embroidered with threads of gold. She lay there, daydreaming under the warm brightness of the sun and the cotton softness of the clouds~ wishing that she could not hear her mothers' voice in the distant lands of her home~ calling on her to come back and complete the evening's chores.

When they grew up- at times- usually they married. At times, he or she passed away from old age or some unlikely tragedy. Sometimes they were joined in holy matrimony with others whom they were forced to betroth through custom, family covenant or possession of the right hand. Other times, they fulfilled less than illustrious desires, spent time alone, lonely or simply wished that they could spend a lifetime together, *once again*. Life to them seemed to be an endless cycle of change and a continual lesson in a book.

This was the usual story. It had been so for eons, as they traveled down the well-paved streets of Atlantis, or as she danced for him under the stars and perfumed breath of Lotus blossoms on the steps of the Taj Mahal; sacredly anointed themselves in Ancient Khemet with Frankincense and Myrrh, bathing together in Golden Vats of milk and sandalwood or washing themselves in the Black Sea or was it the Aegean or Nile?

She lost track of the times, places and faces, but she knew him and recognized him in all his glory…

At times he was her mother, *then her father*. At other times he was her brother, *then her sister*. Once he was a stranger who had no eyes, but through wise insight *made her see*. Then, as if returning a kind favor, he was her guide, her spirit guide, drifting faithfully by her side, steadily directing her through streets she bumped through or on the back of faithful donkeys, when she could not see, *or so she thought*…

Now she was not blind, nor was he a stranger. She saw him in his glory, and knew him well…

He called her on her cell phone and spoke of wondrous things~ he still had a way with words. She pranced around her kitchen making vegetable soup and singing something or the other from Luther or India.Arie, happily. He inspired her to *Be*…

The sun excitedly warmed her back as she walked to meet him in a nearby park. Its' rays tickled her playfully, feeling her anticipation; they danced upon her neck and shone gladness in through her heart. The trees, at first sight, studied her gingerly, then, upon apperception tenderly hummed harmoniously, while the flowers outstretched their petals forcing fine mists of their essence wafting through the air, delightfully perfuming her pathway, stimulating her olfactory~ radiantly enhancing her beauty~ inspiring the pep in her step!

When she found the bench that he spoke of, she noticed that a leaf had thoughtfully landed in the place where she had envisioned herself gracefully nestled. It was a green maple leaf with sugared edges. She carefully placed it in the book she had been carrying, pulled out her canvas and oils to paint.

She had just completed the womb of her woman when he quietly sat down beside her, peered at her painting and happily exclaimed, "Nice! So you paint too, huh?"
Her cheeks warmed. A smile escaped her lips as she nodded and whispered, "Yes, I paint too…"
Each stole side glances at the other, careful not to peer in each others' eyes, fearing to get lost.

"Peace Beloved!" He proclaimed as an afterthought, enthusiastically.

"Peace…" She replied, as a bird fluttered its wings and landed on the branch of the old Maple tree, all within earshot, witnessing their behavior.

"So, What are you doing this lifetime?"
He watched her complete the golden honey Queen on her canvas, all the while determining if this was symbolic of her current journey or of a less than distant past.

"I'm painting, as you can see. Traveling, paying bills, tryin' to enjoy life and survive- you?"

She wished she could watch his lips as he spoke, but the bird chided her in song to remain steadfast and strong and, well…keep painting…

"I'm busy this time around…*very*." He paused to take a laborious breath, then continued slowly, lightly chuckling as he stated,

"I've been married twice, *unhappily*, divorced the last one and vowed to take my time, *the next time*…"

"Hmmm…" She listened attentively & smiled, and painted. The tone of his voice was low and sad, carefully masked behind a demeanor of light-hearted pleasantries.

Then as if tired of the façade, he exhaled, peered up at the sky then sighed quietly,
"I work many jobs now, have to, to keep busy, so I won't focus on my pain…"
He turned to face her, then asked, "How about you?"

She couldn't find an answer to that. Thoughtfully, she painted quietly as she decided what to share and what to withhold- fearing she would give away too much, too soon- of what could easily be saved for future walks on the beach or late nights under the moon and stars, after the children were in bed…
"I've been separated for a few years. As to marriage? I'm working on my divorce now…"

The strokes of her brush steadily mimicked the rise and fall of her voice.

She continued carefully,

"I can't really work like I desire with the children and all, since I have so many fires burning and two hands to tend them. When I have time, I like to paint, sing and write poetry. It allows me to think and be at rest. I love to travel, *still haven't lost that desire yet…*"

Her words struck a chord. He chuckled to himself, sadly, as her words brought back to mind how she disappeared in that caravan, across the *Tanezrouft* [8]…

Disappeared, into the blood red rays of the retiring sun. *Vanished…*

She apprehensively offered him her hands, then, peering for the first time into his eyes, promised to return to him after her journey. Solemnly vowed to fulfill her word to wed him after appeasing burning insatiable desires to journey into distant lands, behold strange people, eat exotic foods, imbibe majestic elixirs and feast on landscapes of strange animals.

Lovingly she squeezed his hands and held them firmly, then excitedly turned from him, picking up her running off to the awaiting camel train, pausing long enough to peer back and flash a pearly smile, before being helped onto her camel and secured carefully on her *hawdaj* [9] for what she anticipated would be an arduous, yet exciting trip. As the caravan departed she peered out and waved from beneath the canopy of her hawdaj and signaled to him that she would soon return.

She never did. Long after the full moon graciously transformed itself through her various faces into a crescent moon- finally re-birthing itself into a new moon- they ventured through the desert. After the Moon began to change her face, they finally decided to stop their journey for several days that made her feel like it was months, hydrating themselves and outstretching their limbs in silken tents under a brilliantly starry sky.

---

[8] The Tanezrouft is one of the most desolate parts of the Sahara Desert, bordering along the countries of Algeria, Niger and Mali. It is west of the Hoggar Mountains.

[9] Hawdaj: Arabic for "Litter," "Houdah", which is a portable seat that is secured on the back of elephants, camels or other animals for easy transport. They were used in Africa, India and Asia by the wealthy or affluent families of those societies, and were adorned with precious jewels to denote the wealth and status of its' occupant.

Then, late into one night, long after the watchmen drifted into a drunken stupor, a band of thieves attacked them. Under half a moon within their travels- across those hot, blistering sands- they slaughtered all the men and young boys who fought them, then gathered the women and children for their own sadistic pleasures, tying their hands and feet together and throwing them on the backs of their camel train. Choosing to keep some and selling those that were younger and would bring a good price to the pale skinned toubab[10] with blue piercing eyes and a foul odor that reminded one of rotting meat...

That was the last he had seen or heard of her. The Elders said that she and all with her had been carried away to a land far beyond the edge of their waters.

Far, far away they traveled, to a land where the eagles gathered over a carcass and feasted delightfully for four hundred years.

His only comfort at the time, in between bleeding tears and the thought of death's salutation, was in the fact that now she would really travel, as her heart had so desperately desired. Travel far to a strange, distant place, among a strange people, in a land that was not hers.

His only regret was that he had refused to join her on that journey, choosing instead to complete his studies in Timbuktu, a promise made to his father to continue apprenticing as a scribe for the Temple until he had fulfilled his mother's last wishes.

He remembered thinking that if he were present at the moment of the ambush- he would have fought valiantly- skillfully using his sword to remove the heads of the attackers, all in the name of protecting his Beloved!

He watched her paint her golden Queen, then sighed- relieved she was still so very beautiful- her breath still smelling of cloves and rosewater.

---

10 Toubab: A term commonly used in Central and West Africa for people of European descent, meaning "white people" or "white devil".

"Is it four o'clock yet?" she asked, remembering the ambush and the terror that stopped her heart for centuries.

"Almost... Ready, to eat?"
He asked, glancing at his watch, careful not to startle her steady hand as she completed the feet of her golden Goddess.

"Yes." She replied, quickly gathering her brushes and tubes of paint, carefully placing them in a case by her feet.

They chose a table out under the clear blue sky. The trees carefully lowered their leaf-laden heads, bending in closer to shade some of the sun off of their skin.

"The salad will be fine, as long as it has a lot of dark green leafy vegetables. I *need that* chlorophyll!"

Playfully, she said this to a waiter who seemed less than interested in her conversation and more concerned with trying to remember her special requests- *no meat, no mushrooms, no nuts*- a lot of things to accomplish a meal *par excellence!*~

"I'll have the same..." he chimed in, "Just add some spinach to my garden burger, please..."

She knew that he didn't eat any more meat. She was glad to see that they were both on the same page. Nothing had changed. Only the place, time and their faces. Nothing else. They were growing together, *still*, just like they had promised the Creator of the Universe, so many trillions of years before...

Stevie Wonder's "Ribbon in the Sky" was the backdrop to their early spring rendezvous. She sang the words inaudibly, still too shy to sing in front of him~ choosing instead to remain quiet, learning more about him and herself~ an *alluring mystery*.

She attentively listened as he shared stories of his own travels. At times she laughed with him, delightfully throwing back her head allowing her joy to freely escape her lips, kissing the sun in ecstasy; or fought to hold back saltwater tears, wishing she could have been there to comfort and nurture him during the bitter, lachrymose times. By the time their meal had arrived, he shared a tender portion of himself that was reminiscent of her own.

It was as if she were *watching* herself, as a man, gracefully dancing through life's carefully choreographed, yet unexpected twists and turns- shimmying, strutting, careening and shindigging- even catching a quick breath, then taking a moment to rhumba or conga his way through each conundrum … and she loved the picture! He was indeed her sacred twin.

She ate the food delightfully, *deliberately,* carefully savoring each bite, wishing that the hands of time would slow to a grinding halt and stand by, attentively watching without judgment or questions- just stand at attention and observe- not daring to move until she commanded it to do so…

It was not so. It could not be so. So, very soon it was time for them both to say "goodbye" retiring reluctantly to their own homes. She, to her makeshift family of exuberant fatherless children. He, to an empty room with hollow walls and painful memories…

"So, shall we meet again?" she asked breezily, "I have Yoga on Mondays and Wednesdays, but outside of my Studies at the Temple on Friday and *doing for self,* I have the ability to make some days *free*…"
She spoke as a seasoned diplomat, carefully choosing words, shielding a burning desire to sit under the watchful eyes of the moon and trees, conversing with him again…

"Sounds like a plan to me…" He careened into her thoughts and cooled the fire of her fantasy,
"Let me look at my schedule first, then we can plan another reunion, or, better yet, I will see you at the Temple and we can make our arrangements from there…"
He covered his smile, happy that she was willing to see him again. Secretly desiring that she might feel more comfortable with being around him, hoping to inspire her to spend another lifetime with him.
"Ok. Sounds good…" She pleasantly broke his thoughts,
 "I'll call you when I arrive home, I'm just up this block here, but, all the neighbors know me, so I'll be fine…"

Although she knew he was obligated to, she didn't want to invite him to walk her home at this time. Not today, as she preferred to reminisce on his memoirs and reflect quietly on the gentility of his spirit…

"Peace Beloved!" He stated kindly,
"Peace…" she replied, waving slowly and turned to walk away.

Suddenly conscious of her movements, she was careful not to throw her hips or stumble on a stone. Careful not to glance back and see if it were his eyes that she felt, softly gazing upon her, securing her, making sure that she had arrived at her destination unscathed. By the time her eyes fell upon the door to her home, *she knew.*

Breathlessly she had the desire to run, then walk, then fly, *up, up! And away~!* Skyrocketing into the jet black droplets of crystal ether that canopied the *Wombniverse* just above her head…

He was that Black God that danced with her in the Temple of Tehuti! Danced around her *nineteen times!*, melodically singing his love inscriptions onto the golden scrolls of her heart! Tantalized her with his songs of praise and beauty! Seduced her ears until she passionately promised him that she would indeed spend the rest of her lifetimes with him!

Why? In Essence, it was not only because he had danced around her and tranquilized her spirit, it was also because she *knew him* since the beginning of time *and loved him; he knew and loved her,* and thus, for that very fact she was pleased…
Yes, indeed…
She was *very pleased!*
  …The Beginning…

The Beginning...
Womb Wisdom.

246 *Poetic Anthologies of She*

WÖMB WISDÖM

As WömbMen we are always on the Sacred path, journeying to Self. At times we come across bumps or even fences in the road that may cause us to slow down or even stop. Do not look at these as impediments to our growth, as they simply are doorways that open up to allow other wömbmen to come forth, formulate their tools, share their "womb wisdom" and nurture our expansion into beautiful beings of light. The following quotes are from some of the wömbmen who have served in my own journey. Please study their words and utilize them on your own journey to Self…

"Allow your self to grow up…"
~Queen Afua's powerful advice to me after i completed this book.
August 27, 2014

"Embrace and Celebrate the Universe of You. This is a life-long journey."
Personal Philosophy: Pray. Love. Laugh. Music & Dance. Everyday.
Pedagogical philosophy: Use everything to teach everything.
~ Gerianne Francis Scott, BA, MS., Educator, Editor & Word Artist

"My SiStars, my daughters, it is so very important to know thyself…to know the beauty and the power of your WombHeart. Loving all aspects of your womanhood will help to make the world a better place, when you joyously embrace your first blood, menarche, moving through life to to your Wise Woman years when your Sacred Blood no longer flows forth from your womb. These are rites of passages, not a sickness. Celebrate the stages of your womanhood! Love yourself! You are the circle of life…the web of destiny. You are magnificent!"
~Diva Mama Tonya K. Freeman, Poet, Co-founder of MOSA Radio and host of "Wisdom Talks"

To My Sisters: "Spread your Wisdom- not your legs. Fornication is the End of Days"
It wasn't until I became a woman at the age of 36 that I realized the best love anyone can ever experience is the love of and for ALLAH (God). Then the unconditional love of myself. Finally, I knew that with all the fornication I have done, there was never any love- just a lot of lust and hurt. I was destroying myself, my womb and my nation. So I want to apologize to God, my mother, myself, my ancestors, and all the little boys and girls who witnessed all my sinning ways and thought I was living the life and followed in my footsteps to the belly of negativity (HELL). Sister, I am changing back to the righteous way, come out of HELL with me (you can crawl back out), join me in healing!
~Tosha M. Thomas Muhammad, Ms. Diligent Notary Services, Newburgh, NY

9 stages of WombManHood

There was a man, who was calling on God and constantly asking for help,
Finally one day he called on God and when God answered he said,
"Why didn't you answer me when I called on you?"
God responded,
"I tried to, but every time I called, your line was busy…"

Silence. We must spend time in silence. It is important to dwell in silence and listen. Praise & Thanks… We must praise God and be thankful… Be thankful for His wisdom and knowledge. This is when God can work through you, when you are praising and thanking Him!

~Shirlee' Bannarn, Healer, Advisor & Indigenous Spiritual Mother, Minneapolis, Minnesota

Through my life's journey, I have learned that sisterhood is very important to a woman's growth, spiritually and mentally. A woman has so much power, so never look at your sister as a competitor, but as an extension of feminine power.

~Kellie Constantine, Oakland, CA

The secret to how God created Himself was placed in the woman by the Original God. In that, we see His value of you, the woman, is crucial for His return to his own origin. His return is your return. Allow yourself personal healing that you may be the compass and the light to return the whole of humanity to an existence beyond his original glory. Allow yourself to take in and become one with all that is good and all that is useful. You not only give good and love and life. You are good. You are love. You are life. Find your way home, so that through you, humanity will return. ~Catina Muhammad, St. Louis, MO.

Beautiful Ones, Our journey is an inspiration even though it doesn't feel that way much of the time. Behold, with clarity, and love WHO YOU ARE, Give honor to WHERE YOU COME FROM…Remember how far you have come and what it took to get to this place. Stand Joy-filled in your truth unafraid, for where you are going, the TRUTH shall set you Free!~

~Lisa Simone Kelly, Singer, Healer & daughter of Priestess of Soul Nina Simone, France, August 18, 2014

My life's journey has been extreme but here is what I have learned. I "check in" with myself every day by asking myself what did I do today, if I didn't get to it I forgive myself and add it to the top of the list for tomorrow, what did I do to take care of Tiffany today? I am a nurturer and its easy to forget about myself but in order to nurture those that are sent my way It is important to have self- care. Stay present as much as I can. Auto pilot and "fake it till you make it" are temporary. Self care is a lifestyle change that includes my health, emotional balance, feeding my spirit, and my inner peace. Life is short make it count…Peace and blessings ~Tiffany "Sweet T", Oakland, CA

WOMB WISDOM.
It is the seat of all creation on the planet.
It is the ever-flowing life source.
It is the place where you KNOW,
That you KNOW, that you know….

And it is the place where, when exposed to hatred, abuse and distrust, can shift the path of our lives. Where is this place? It is our WOMBS and within all of our wombs lies our BECKONING, our CALLING, our TRUTH and our UNCONDITIONAL LOVE…. our WOMB WISDOM.

Women, we have been sold a fake bill of goods about our wombs and as such we have lost the true beauty, strength and renewing regeneration that resides within our wombs.

*Every month our wombs remind us that we can take on, build up, marinate, create and then release ideas, love, light, hopes, dreams and visions like no other creatures on the planet. You see, our monthly moon cycles are our internal renewing, our REBIRTH! Our brains (our creative ideas) send a message to our wombs (the light) and our wombs respond by thickening the uterine lining (the build up). Once ovulation occurs, the egg (the creativity seed) travels from the Fallopian tubes and finds the thickened uterus (the marination) and then the menses (the birth of the release, love, hope, dreams and visions) occurs. This indeed is NOT our weakness and unclean time as we have been told, rather it is our MOST SPIRITUALLY, PHYSICALLY, EMOTIONALLY and MENTALLY cleansing and MOST powerful times. It is in these times we should put into motion any positive intentions regarding life, career, love, money, past healing or trauma because it is when we are most connected to ourselves and our Universe! WOMBMAN, listen to your other still small voice, trust your wisdom, embrace your womb, exercise your **WOMB WISDOM**...ALWAYS in all ways."*
~Sandra Thomas, Atlanta, GA, Aug 7, 2013

32 years and counting… many lessons have been revealed. However, the greatest lesson I've learned throughout my life is to "LOVE YOURSELF". If you haven't learned to completely embrace and love yourself you will always be left with a feeling of emptiness and lack. True love begins with you. There was a time in my life when I realized I invested more time and love on my relationships then I did on myself. I felt empty because I set myself up to relay on my relationships to validate my happiness. As women we are natural caretakers. In the mist of our emotions we tend lose ourselves in our mate, family and others, often putting aside our own dreams and aspirations. I feel it's important to spend time alone as woman. If we poured the same love and attention we do in our relationships inward towards ourselves we will gracefully overcame any challenge and rise as high as our hearts desire. As a woman you MUST know who you are and unapologetically LOVE yourself, so in the event you find yourself alone, you will still be complete, full of love and life. The depth of love you are able to give and receive will increase when you learn this great lesson. To maintain our position as Goddesses, its imperative we don't lose ourselves while occupied with others. We must stay grounded which is achieved through self-love. Loving yourself is loving God. Never forget you

are one.

Love, Peace & Light! ~Myriam Boukari, Atlanta, GA

We as WombMen are always absorbing and taking in ideas, energies and realities. We are the Second Self of The Creator, that One who evolved in Triple Darkness. WombMen like her Father, is also creating ideas and realities in the Triple Darkness of her Mind and her Womb. We are Co-Creators with The Creator who created "The Heavens and the Earth." We must awaken and live up to our fullest potential- The Woman of The Cosmic Universe - Rulers of the Heavens and the Earth.

~Sis. Najma Muhammad

Speaking life

What has been profoundly transformative for me has been the knowing that our capacity to give and receive love is directly related to our ability to love our self. We draw to us people and experiences that reflect how we truly feel about ourselves. We began to experience a major shift when we cultivate what I call the art of speaking life. It is important to redefine our relationship with ourselves by speaking life into your cells, your reflection, your water, your food, your mate, your children, your community and your world and your life is transformed. Life begets life. Every positive thought propels you further in the right direction. The proof will be in your amazing relationships, healthy body and fruitful life.

In our true essence, no matter what life has been up until this point, we are a divine spark of light and love. So speak life and shine bright!

With love and gratitude,

~Jennifer Bliss, Atlanta, GA

When Woman looks in the mirror, she must see that she is the very creative essence of the Universe, for from within her all of our questions are ultimately answered, all gains are attained, all blessings are bestowed…It is from her lips that Prophets speak, through her womb that Christ's come and from her lungs that Gods breathe… She is the proverbial bearer of Truth. She is the herald. She is the Angel, and most importantly, she is its Mother.

~ Keenia Farrell, Contractor/Interior Designer, Co-Owner of Chakra Teas Co.

"If we desire to secure Peace, Freedom, Justice and Equality for our people, it will be found in the work, and the work must always start with Self and at Home"

~Sister Shyne, Washington, D.C., S.I.O.N. Another Clean Glass Production~

250 *Poetic Anthologies of She*

The following creed is for the sake of elevating the Feminine Principle not on paper, but within our DNA, which must be reconstructed by way of a change in diet, a change in physical and mental environment, and stimulation by way of conscious effort.

1. *I shall choose my mates wisely, and reproduce responsibly.*
2. *I shall feed my offspring before answering my own call to hunger.*
3. *I shall keep my surrounding clean, free from physical, mental, and spiritual debris.*
4. *I shall protect myself from any and all undesirable elements that ill affect my functionality and alter my performance on any level.*
5. *I shall be a woman of my word never giving it without the intent on following through.*
6. *I shall ensure that my needs are met at ALL times.*
7. *I shall understand that settling is NEVER an option.*
8. *I shall maintain my identity.*
9. *I shall ensure the maintenance of my offspring.*
10. *I shall secure my mental state.*

This is a beginning, a starting point for us to motion our way BACK toward the reality of GOD made manifest within our being. Once we have begun to master these elements, we will begin to notice a shift in our reality. We will no longer feel the need to profess with our mouths that which permeates throughout our reality. Knowledge isn't power until it's applied.

~ Ebony Hotep

9 stages of WombManHood

WRITE YOUR WÖMB WISDÖM HERE...

252 *Poetic Anthologies of She*

ÄBOUT SHË

Dr. Tisa Farrell-Muhammad
Author & Illustrator

As Author of 9 stäges of WömbManHood, Dr. Muhammad, a native of Toronto, Ontario, Canada, is a seasoned advocate for Wömb-Wellness and Wömen's Empowerment, focusing her attention on educating women and their families on issues of health, wealth, happiness and wellness.

As Founder and Visionary of A Phoenix Rising Wellness Institute (www.aprwi.com), she implements programs regularly that fulfill her lifelong mission of service through being a true tool of the Creator of the Wömbniverse.

Dr. Tisa holds a B.S. in Orthomolecular Medicine (Natural Nutritional Medicine), and is qualified as a Doctor of Natural Medicine, Vibrational Medicine and a Doctor of Homeopathic Medicine (Canadian College of Humanitarian Medicine). She is also a Wömb Counselor, Medical Intuitive, Certified Clinical Iridologist (Canadian Institute of Iridology), and a Certified Holistic Healthcare Consultant trained by World-Renown Healer, Author and Lecturer, Dr. Llaila O. Afrika.

As a Medical Artist she has dedicated herself to the Cultural Revolution combining all of the Arts, in an effort to assist in holistically healing all members of the human family. Through years of service, Dr. Muhammad has had the honor of visiting Russia, Cuba, Europe and the Caribbean, where she has had the opportunity to study different cultures and languages.

Through the gift of song and theatrical arts, with over twenty-five years of stage performances, she has utilized her gifts as a Vibrational Therapist, applying the healing principles of sound and breath for transformative purposes to her clients.

In addition, Dr. Muhammad organizes Lectures/Workshops focusing on Wömb Wellness, Wholistic

Vibrational Arts, Past Life Regressions, Wömb Journeying as well as other areas in the Whölistic Medical Arts!

Currently she is focusing her attention on the principles of **How to Eat to Live,** as taught by the Most Hon. Elijah Muhammad, as part of her dedicated pursuit to transform the health of every member of the human family. In the midst of it all, she is the proud, dedicated mother of seven beautiful, intelligent and patient children.

www.ingramcontent.com/pod-product-compliance
Lightning Source LLC
Chambersburg PA
CBHW041150290426
44108CB00002B/29